UKULELE

A FUN AND SIMPLE GUIDE TO PLAYING UKULELE

by Chad Johnson

PLAYBACK+
Speed • Pitch • Balance • Loop

To access audio visit:
www.halleonard.com/mylibrary

Enter Code
7801-8292-1822-2570

Front cover photos courtesy of Flight Instruments

ISBN 978-1-4950-9374-6

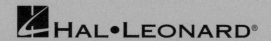

Visit Hal Leonard Online at
www.halleonard.com

Contact us:
Hal Leonard
7777 West Bluemound Road
Milwaukee, WI 53213
Email: info@halleonard.com

In Europe, contact:
Hal Leonard Europe Limited
42 Wigmore Street
Marylebone, London, W1U 2RN
Email: info@halleonardeurope.com

In Australia, contact:
Hal Leonard Australia Pty. Ltd.
4 Lentara Court
Cheltenham, Victoria, 3192 Australia
Email: info@halleonard.com.au

T0088805

FUNNY STUFF

Q: What's "perfect pitch"?
A: When you throw a ukulele into the garbage can without hitting the rim.

Q: What is the difference between a ukulele and an onion?
A: Nobody cries when you cut up a ukulele.

Q: How many ukulele players does it take to change a lightbulb?
A: Ten—one to change the bulb and nine to say how much better Jake Shimabukuro would have done it.

Q: What do a ukulele and a lawsuit have in common?
A: Everyone is happy when the case is closed.

Q: If you're lost wandering in the desert, what do you aim for: a good ukulele player, a bad ukulele player, or an oasis?
A: The bad ukulele player. The other two are only figments of your imagination.

Q: Why shouldn't you drive off a cliff in a golf cart with three ukuleles in it?
A: You could fit at least five more in the cart.

Q: What do you call a beautiful woman on a ukulele player's arm?
A: A tattoo.

Q: Why are band breaks limited to only 20 minutes?
A: So you don't have to retrain the ukulele player.

Q: Why aren't banjo ukuleles popular?
A: They take twice as long to burn.

Q: What is the difference between a ukulele and a trampoline?
A: People take their shoes off to jump on a trampoline.

A ukulele player suddenly realizes he left his vintage ukulele in his car overnight. He rushes outside and his heart drops when he sees that his car window is broken. Fearing the worst, he peeks through the window and finds that there are now five ukuleles in his car.

BRIEF CONTENTS

FULL CONTENTS

Page   Track

INTRODUCTION

Is there any instrument that brings as much unadulterated joy as the ukulele? It's a scientific fact: it's very hard to be sad when you hear someone strumming a uke. (OK, maybe it's not scientifically proven, but it should be!) It's no wonder that the instrument has made a huge comeback over the past decade, as millions have come to appreciate its wealth of musical goodness. What instrument is better-suited for a hike? What other instrument sounds like a bubbling brook when you strum the open strings? What other instrument has such an awesome name? That would be the uke, folks!

If you have some experience with the instrument and want to further your studies, or if you've never even touched one before but are ready to see what all the fuss is about, you've come to the right place. Even though the instrument is small, the world of the ukulele is wide and vast, and there's something in this book for everyone. I truly hope you enjoy working through it as much as I did writing it!

—Chad Johnson, 2019

ABOUT THIS BOOK

All About Ukulele is primarily aimed at the beginning ukulele player, although there's plenty of material here for intermediate players, as well. But we'll start from ground zero to get the greenest of beginners up and running. Once up and running, the pace of the book will pick up a bit in order to cover the vast array of topics encased within. Because of this, if you're a true beginner, it's a good idea to partner this book with another beginner's guide until you've thoroughly mastered the basics. While this book starts with baby steps, it also features plenty of material into which you can grow as your progress continues on the instrument.

We'll also discuss the practical side of the instrument, including selecting the right uke and things to keep in mind for a gig. We'll talk about the big-name players who have influenced us all and list essential recordings to check out. And, along with numerous examples and exercises, most of which are featured on the included audio, we'll also make use of real songs to illustrate the techniques and concepts you'll be learning throughout. In fact, toward the end of the book, you'll find full-length transcriptions of five songs—demonstrating a wide variety of uke techniques—that are also included on the audio.

Is Reading Music Necessary?

The short answer to this question? A little. You certainly don't need to be able to sight-read notes. And whatever reading you do need to perform will be covered in detail. In fact, many of the examples use a shorthand form of notation called *rhythm slashes*, whereby you only need to be able to read the rhythms. And when you are playing melodies and other examples that feature standard music notation, they will be paired with another type of notation called *tablature*, or "tab" for short, which is a very user-friendly visual aid that makes reading a cinch. Additionally, most of the examples in the book are performed on the accompanying audio so you can always have a listen to check your accuracy. In short, you will develop some music-reading skills as you work through this book, but it won't be a painful procedure in the least.

Follow these guidelines when working through the book:

* **Study the pictures and diagrams that accompany most new chord shapes and scales, etc.** These are a valuable resource that can speak volumes, especially for visual learners.
* **Follow the tablature when present.** This easy-to-follow notation will tell you which strings to play and where to place your fingers on the fretboard.

- **Listen to the accompanying audio tracks.** Even if you're able to read an example, it's a good idea to listen to the tracks to hear if you're catching all the subtleties of the music. Additionally, the audio can work wonders for clearing up a tricky rhythm that's giving you problems.

- **If you desire, you can begin paying more attention to the music staff as you progress through the book.** This is not necessary to perform the material. In fact, many famous musicians can't read a lick of music. However, if you find yourself wanting to learn how, then it'll be there for you to study.

Which Ukulele Do I Need?

The material in this book can be performed on any type of ukulele that has four strings and is in standard tuning: G–C–E–A. This includes soprano, concert, and tenor models. The one difference that may occur depends on whether you use the standard *reentrant* tuning or not. This is the typical "My Dog Has Fleas" ukulele tuning in which the fourth string is tuned above the pitch of the third string (and above the second string, as well). A thinner string is used for this purpose. However, some people prefer to tune their ukes—particularly the tenor uke—to "low G," which requires the use of a thicker fourth string so that it can be tuned an octave lower than in reentrant tuning. The notes will all be the same regardless of the tuning, but the effect will be quite different depending on the octave of the G string.

All of the examples in this book were designed with standard, reentrant tuning in mind, and that's how all the audio tracks were recorded. But many of the examples will sound just fine in low G tuning, as well. Note that a baritone ukulele is an exception, as it sounds lower in pitch than standard uke models and is therefore not compatible with this method.

ABOUT THE AUDIO

Most of the examples in this book are present on the accompany audio, which can be streamed or downloaded by following the instructions on page 1. Throughout the book, an audio icon will designate which examples are recorded and on which track they can be found.

When backing instruments appear on a track, the ukulele will be mixed on the right side and the other instruments will be on the left. This will allow you to either examine the ukulele by itself or completely remove it from the mix for play-along purposes by adjusting the balance control on your stereo. If you are streaming the audio, you can use the *PLAYBACK+* audio player to pan the balance left or right. If you're wearing headphones and don't have a balance control, you can simply remove one headphone to hear the part you want.

Each example is preceded by four clicks called a "count-off," which lets you know the proper tempo. Think of it as a very precisely-timed "ready, set, go!" Most examples will have four clicks, but examples in 3/4 time will have three clicks, and so on.

EXPLANATION OF COMMON TERMS

As you work through this book, you'll come across several terms repeatedly. Here is a list of these terms and their definitions.

- **Higher:** This usually refers to pitch rather than geography. In other words, the "highest string" on the uke is string 1 (the thinnest), even though it's closest to the floor. This is because it's the highest pitched of them all. The uke is a bit of an exception in this regard because the third string is actually the lowest-pitched string (instead of the fourth) due to the reentrant tuning. Nevertheless, "higher" will also refer to moving along a string toward the bridge.

- **Lower:** This is the opposite of higher and refers to going down in pitch. This can refer to moving from string 1 to string 2 or moving from fret 5 to fret 3 along a string.

- **Right and Left Hands:** Although we know there are lefty uke players out there, for the sake of simplicity, we'll stick with the right-hand perspective. So, in this book, the "right hand" describes the strumming or plucking hand. The "left hand" describes the fretting hand. If you're a left-handed player, just reverse these right/left directives any time you see them.
- **Ukulele:** The word "ukulele" (or "uke") in this book always refers to a soprano, concert, or tenor uke in reentrant tuning.

ICON LEGEND

You'll see several icons located in the left margins throughout the book. These draw your attention to specific topics and help you navigate through the book. Here's a list and a description of these icons:

AUDIO
This icon accompanies the music examples. The number on the icon corresponds to the audio track.

TRY THIS
This includes helpful advice about various aspects of ukulele playing.

EXTRAS
Here, you'll find additional information on a variety of topics that you may find interesting and useful, but not necessarily essential.

DON'T FORGET
This book includes a wealth of information that may prove difficult to remember. This icon marks short refresher lessons that will help you stay the course.

DANGER!
Playing the ukulele can, in some ways, be physically demanding. These tips will help you avoid injury and also help prevent you from developing bad habits that would hinder your progress.

ORIGINS
Here, you'll find interesting and fun historical blurbs.

NUTS & BOLTS
Included with this icon are tidbits on the fundamentals or building blocks of music.

Preparation

CHAPTER 1
GETTING TO KNOW YOUR UKULELE

> ***What's Ahead:***
> - Parts of the ukulele
> - How ukuleles work
> - How ukuleles are played

In this first section, you're going to learn the ins and outs of your ukulele. After all, you're going to share an intimate relationship with your instrument, so it's good to take some time to familiarize yourself with its parts and workings. We'll talk about the construction of the uke, its parts, how it's played, how it's tuned, and other important preparatory tidbits. Additionally, we'll cover some tips on practicing to help you make the most of the time you spend with the uke in your hands.

If you bought this book before purchasing a uke, then jump to Section 6 and read through it thoroughly before taking a trip to the music store. This will allow you to make a more educated purchase, ensuring that you actually get what you want. If you already have a uke on hand (be it new or a hand-me-down), then let's get down to business.

PARTS OF THE UKULELE
The photo on the adjacent page illustrates all the parts on a common uke and is preceded below by a brief description of each.

Body: This is essentially the sound chamber that amplifies the sound of the ukulele's vibrating strings. It's commonly made out of mahogany, koa, spruce, or acacia woods.

Bridge: This is a wooden piece attached to the body that anchors the strings at one end.

Frets: These metal wires are embedded in the fretboard and lay perpendicular to the strings. These are used to produce the different pitches along a string.

Headstock: This serves as the end of the neck and contains the tuning pegs, which anchor the other end of the strings.

Inlays (Fret Markers): These markers help you keep your place along the fretboard. On the ukulele, they commonly appear at frets 5, 7, 10, and 12. (Note that this is different from a guitar or bass, where they normally appear at frets 3, 5, 7, 9, and 12.)

Neck and Fretboard: The neck is the long, wooden piece along which the strings run. It's commonly made from the same woods used for the back and sides. The fretboard is a thin slab of wood along the top of the neck, commonly made from rosewood or ebony.

Nut: This thin strip separates the headstock from the fretboard. Commonly made from plastic or bone, it features grooves that hold the strings in place.

Saddle: Similar to the nut, the saddle is also commonly made from plastic or bone. The strings make contact with the saddle just before being anchored (tied) to the bridge.

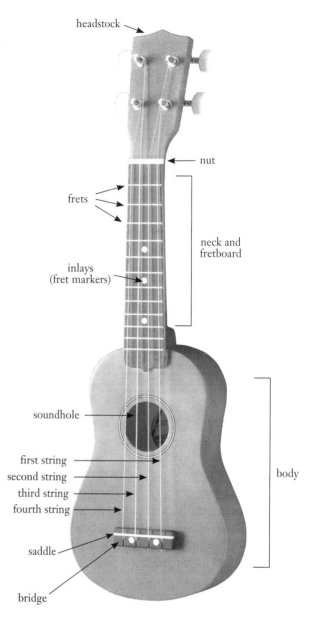

Soundhole: This is a hole in the body of the ukulele designed to project the sound.

Fourth string: The fourth string is the one that's closest to the ceiling while in playing position. On a soprano (standard uke), it's tuned to a G note and is actually the second-thinnest string.

Third string: The third string is actually the thickest, lowest-pitched string on a standard-tuned soprano uke. It's tuned to C.

Second string: The second string is tuned to the note E.

First string: The first string is the one closest to the floor while in playing position. It's the thinnest string and is tuned to the note A.

HOW UKULELES WORK

A uke principally works by projecting the volume of vibrating strings. Just as a rubber band will make a pitch when you stretch and pluck it, so does the uke. The headstock (and specifically, the tuning pegs) anchor the strings at one end, and the bridge anchors them at the other end. The top piece of the body, which is called the *soundboard*, vibrates when a string is plucked, causing the entire body to resonate and amplify the sound. By pressing the strings down at certain frets, you're shortening or increasing the length of the vibrating strings, thus making the pitch higher or lower, respectively.

origins

The ukulele's beginnings can be roughly traced to the 1880s in Hawaii. Based off several Portuguese instruments, including the machete, cavaquinho, and the rajão, the first ukuleles are generally credited to three immigrant cabinet makers: Manuel Nunes, José do Espírito Santo, and Augusto Dias. The instrument quickly became imbedded in Hawaiian culture, due largely in part to King Kala-kaua, who frequently incorporated it into royal gatherings and concerts.

The uke began to spread throughout the world by the early 1900s, first appearing in the U.S. mainland in 1915 around San Francisco, where it gained popularity via the Royal Hawaiian Quartet, as well as Jonah Kumalae. By the 1930s, it had reached Japan by way of Hawaiian Yukihiko Haida, who'd journeyed there after his Japanese father had died. Haida went on to form the successful Moana Glee Club. Concurrently, the uke made its way to England, where it was greatly popularized by George Formby throughout the 1940s.

HOW THE UKULELE IS PLAYED

The Strings and Their Relationship to Pitch

The four strings on the uke are all tuned to a different pitch. The thinner the string, the higher the pitch. Because of reentrant tuning (see Chapter 2 for more on this), the fourth string is not the thickest and lowest-pitched string on the uke. This is contradictory to most four-stringed instruments, such as the bass guitar, mandolin, or violin. However, it's one of the things that makes the uke sound so unique. To create sound on the uke, you pluck or strum the strings most often with a finger, although people occasionally use a pick (or plectrum) to pluck or strum the strings, as well.

What Do the Frets Do?

Because it's not practical to retune a string every time you want a different pitch, the uke has many frets along the length of the strings. When you press a string down behind a fret, the string makes contact with it, thereby shortening the length of string that's allowed to vibrate and thus raising the pitch. With frets on each string, it's possible to play all kinds of musical intervals up and down the neck. Each fret on each string represents the musical interval of a half step. In other words, when you move up or down one string, fret by fret, it's the same as playing every key (white and black) on a piano keyboard in one direction.

A Two-Handed Job

When playing the ukulele, both hands work together, each focusing on independent skills. The fret hand (left hand for a right-handed player) pushes down frets on different strings to create all the different pitches. The plucking hand (right hand for a right-handed player) creates the rhythm by plucking or strumming the strings. By working together, you create all the different chords and/or melodies possible on the uke.

don't forget

- The three basic parts of the ukulele are the *body*, *neck*, and *headstock*.
- The more tension on a string, the higher the pitch. The lower the tension, the lower the pitch.
- The thinner the string, the higher the pitch. The thicker the string, the lower the pitch.
- The third string is actually the lowest-pitched string on a standard uke.
- Inlays usually appear on frets 5, 7, 10, and 12 of the uke, although there are exceptions. These markers help you keep track of your place on the fretboard.

CHAPTER 2
GETTING IN TUNE

What's Ahead:
* Names and pitches of the open strings
* Using the accompanying audio to tune your uke
* Using an electronic tuner to tune your uke
* Using a piano or keyboard to tune your uke
* Tuning the uke to itself
* Other tuning methods

Many instruments—the violin immediately comes to mind—are capable of some of the most beautiful music in the world, as well as some of the most hideous noises. While the quality of the instrument certainly plays a part, by far the more operative variable is that of the musician playing it. The ukulele is no different in this regard; it can sound beautiful in one person's hands and not so much in another's (although it's hard to top the "nails on a chalkboard" sound that a violin can produce in the hands of a beginner!).

One of the most important factors in creating a pleasant sound on the ukulele is getting the instrument *in tune*. Whereas it's comparatively difficult to knock a piano out of tune, all it takes on a uke is one quick twist of a tuning peg for things to go awry (just ask my five-year-old daughter about this!). Learning to tune can be a bit frustrating if the uke is your first instrument and you haven't developed a good ear yet. But it's an absolutely essential skill if you want your uke playing to sound pleasant; there's just no way around it. Fortunately, there are several tools available to help you out.

THE OPEN STRINGS

The String Numbers

The strings of the uke are each assigned a number, which can be a helpful reference. It's important to memorize this information up front because it will be used throughout the book. The first string (or string 1) is the one nearest to the floor when in playing position. The fourth string (string 4) is nearest to the ceiling. On most string instruments, string 1 would be the thinnest string, and string 4 would be the thickest. On a soprano (standard) uke, however, this is not the case. It uses a tuning system called *reentrant tuning*, whereby the fourth string is tuned one octave higher than normal. Because of this, a thinner gauge string is used for the fourth string, which means that string 3 is actually the thickest (and therefore lowest-pitched) string.

Note Names of the Open Strings

Each open string is tuned to a different pitch, which is assigned a note name. The notes are as follows:

First string: A
Second string: E
Third string: C
Fourth string: G

As with the string numbers, it helps to memorize these note names as soon as possible. If it helps, you can use a mnemonic device, such as: **G**roovy **C**ows **E**at **A**pples, or **G**iant **C**rabs with **E**longated **A**ntennae.

TUNING YOUR UKULELE WITH THE ACCOMPANYING AUDIO

A tuning track on the accompanying audio contains pitches of the four open strings, each played four times. Short of having a private instructor giving you the pitches in person, this is the best source. It'll take a bit of practice to get the tuning method down, but once you get the hang of it, you won't have to think twice about it.

Here's what you do: The first pitch you'll hear will be the open fourth string, G. Immediately after hearing this note, pluck your open fourth string. If you hear a difference in pitch, this means your string is not in tune; it's either *sharp* (too high) or *flat* (too low). Sometimes it's difficult to tell at first whether it's sharp or flat. Regardless, it's a good habit to always tune a string up to pitch instead of down to it. This helps the string hold its tuning better. So, if the string sounds out of tune, always loosen it first. If it seems to move further away from the target pitch, then your string was most likely flat. If it seems to move closer to the target pitch, then your string was most likely sharp. If this is the case, go ahead and detune the string until it's flat and then tune it up to pitch.

When you get your string close to being in tune, you'll begin to hear a wavering sound. These fluctuations are called *beats*. The closer you get to being in tune, the further apart the beats will sound. When they disappear completely, you're in tune. Again, it may take a bit of practice to recognize this sound, but the more you do it, the quicker you'll get.

Each string will be played four times. If you still don't have a string in tune after the fourth time it's played, simply rewind the track to hear it again. Once you finish tuning all four strings, it's a good idea to check them all again. If your uke was severely out of tune, it may take a few times before the tuning settles into place.

TUNING YOUR UKULELE WITH A PIANO OR KEYBOARD

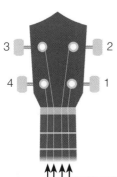

As an alternative to the tuning pitches on the accompanying audio, you can use a piano or keyboard to provide your reference pitches. The process is basically the same; you want to match each string of the uke to the reference pitch, tuning up to pitch instead of down to it. The illustration below demonstrates which keys on the piano to use for tuning purposes.

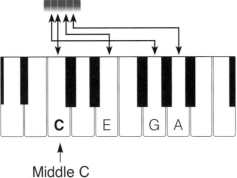

Middle C

You can start with middle C, which is the same pitch as the third string. Play the note on the piano and then pluck your open third string. Use the same procedure to tune the string as you did in the previous method with the accompanying audio. After it's in tune, move to the E (second) string, then the A (first string), and finally the G (fourth) string, remembering that its reference pitch is right next to the A reference for string 1.

You can use the sustain pedal on the piano or keyboard to make it easier on yourself. This will sustain the piano note so you have both hands free for tuning your uke strings.

TUNING YOUR UKULELE WITH AN ELECTRONIC TUNER

The quickest and easiest method of tuning your uke is to use an *electronic tuner*. There are hundreds of electronic tuners on the market, many of which are perfectly suitable for a uke. I highly recommend getting a *chromatic tuner*, which means it can detect the pitch of any note (non-chromatic tuners can usually only recognize certain pitches, such as the pitches of the six strings on a guitar). Most are battery powered, commonly using AA, AAA, or smaller disc-shaped watch batteries, such as a CR2032.

Unless you have an acoustic/electric ukulele (which will have a pickup of some sort and an output jack), you'll need to make sure that the tuner can be used with acoustic instruments. This will mean it's either equipped with an onboard microphone or that it's a *clip-on tuner*. The latter is equipped with a spring-action clamp, allowing you to clamp it to the headstock. Clip-ons are especially convenient, as you can take them anywhere and you don't have to worry about being close enough to the mic. They're also not affected by a noisy environment, which is a big plus.

To use an electronic tuner, simply pluck a string and watch the display. It will indicate which note is being played and also whether it's in tune, sharp, or flat (and by how much). Each tuner's display is slightly different, but they're all fairly intuitive (consult the manual if necessary). Be sure to read what note it's displaying while tuning! That may sound obvious, but it's easy, for example, to focus only on whether it's telling you the string is sharp or flat and ignore the fact that you're tuning your (severely sharp) third string to a C♯ instead of C!

It should be mentioned that there are also dozens of tuning apps for smartphones these days—quite handy for when you don't have your electronic tuner nearby.

Snark ST-2
clip-on tuner

TUNING YOUR UKULELE TO ITSELF

If it's just you and your ukulele all by your lonesome, with no piano, tuner, smartphone (it could happen), or other sound source available, you can still get the uke in tune with itself. This process is called *relative tuning*, and it's a very useful skill to develop. The idea is to tune an open string to a fretted note on another string.

Tips for Getting Close

If you've recently tuned your uke to a tuner or a piano—within a week or so—and the strings aren't brand new, you can probably assume that you're at a good enough starting point. You can then pick one of the strings to be your reference and proceed to the method described on the next page. If, however, you've just restrung the instrument or picked it up after a few months or more, then you'll have to do your best to get one of the strings close enough.

I recommend learning the key of a song that you like and identifying a specific pitch in that song. It's really helpful if you can find a song with an identifiable C, E, A, or G note. For example, the Beatles song "I Want to Hold Your Hand" opens with two E notes on "**Oh, yeah**, I…" If you have that song in your head pretty well, you can hum that note and tune your second string to it. So, your first homework assignment is to find a song that you know well and from which you can identify one of those reference pitches: C, E, G, or A. Below are a few other suggestions:

- **"Rhiannon" by Fleetwood Mac:** In the chorus, the name "Rhiannon" is held out on a long E note.
- **"Iris" by the Goo Goo Dolls:** In the chorus, the first line ("And I **don't want the world**…") consists of several A notes in a row.
- **"Brown Eyed Girl" by Van Morrison:** The high note in the chorus ("**You** my brown-eyed girl") is a G note.
- **"Soul Man" by Sam & Dave:** The title in the chorus ("I'm a **soul man**!") is sung on a G note.
- **"Like a Rolling Stone" by Bob Dylan:** The verse begins by repeating a C note over and over ("**Once upon** a **time**, you **dressed so fine**…")

Matching Fretted Notes to Open Strings

Once you have one string close to what you think is in tune, you can proceed with the method. Here's the basic idea: The note of each open string (with the exception of the third string) can be played as a fretted note on another string:

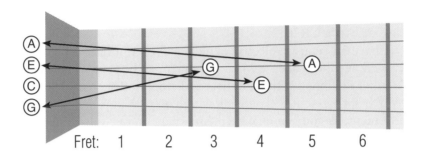

So, for example, let's say you think your second string (E) is close to being in tune. You would proceed as follows:

- Play fret 5 on string 2 (an A note) and then tune the first string until it matches this pitch.

- Play fret 3 on string 2 (a G note) and then tune the fourth string until it matches this pitch.

- Play fret 4 on string 3 (an E note) and then play the open second string. Tune the third string so that its fourth-fret note matches the open second string.

If another one of your strings is the starting pitch, simply adjust as needed, using the same system.

If you want to hear both notes ringing at the same time, you can reach over and turn the peg with your right hand while your left hand stays on the note.

This method will at least get your uke sounding good on its own, even though it may not be exactly in tune with a tuner. As mentioned earlier, this is an excellent skill to develop. Not only is it useful for those times when you're without a tuner or sound source, but it's also fantastic ear training. Learning to tune the instrument on your own is one of the best ways to start developing your ear.

Keep in mind that, when using this tuning method, there's a good chance you won't be in tune with other instruments that have been tuned with a tuner. So, if someone joins you while you're jamming and asks to play along, you may need to retune by getting a reference pitch from them (or giving a reference pitch to them). It's always good practice to check your collective tuning before playing with another musician.

OTHER WAYS TO TUNE YOUR UKULELE

Aside from the previous methods, there are still a few other ways to get in tune. Two useful ways are with a *pitch pipe* or a *tuning fork*.

A pitch pipe is a small circular device that's fitted with holes all around it. Each hole produces a different pitch when blown. It's similar to a harmonica in both principle and sound. A tuning fork is nice for those who want to go really low tech and old school. They're usually tuned to an A pitch (440 Hz), which is perfect for tuning your first string. You grab them by the handle, whack them on something firm (but not hard like a table—your knee works well), and then listen for the pitch by holding the tines up to your ear. You can usually get them to vibrate by pinching the tines together and releasing them, as well.

To amplify the sound of the ringing tuning fork, try touching the handle end against the soundboard of your ukulele. Or, if you *really* want to hear the pitch, hold the vibrating fork handle with your teeth; you'll hear the pitch in your head!

- The strings are numbered 1 through 4. String 4 is the closest to the ceiling while in playing position.

- The notes of the open strings are as follows: 4 = G, 3 = C, 2 = E, 1 = A.

- Because of reentrant tuning, the fourth string is not the thickest or lowest pitch.

- If a string is flat, you tune it up to pitch. If a string is sharp, it's best to first tune it flat and then bring it back up to pitch, as this will help it hold its tuning better.

- The wavering sounds you hear when two notes are nearly in tune are called beats. The further apart the beats, the closer the notes are to being in tune.

- Relative tuning (tuning without an external sound source or tuner) is great practice, but remember to check your tuning with another musician before playing with them.

- Unless you have perfect pitch, you'll need a tuner or reliable pitch source to tune your uke to standard pitch.

CHAPTER 3
POSTURE, POSTURE, POSTURE!

What's Ahead:
- How to hold the uke
- Hand positions
- Using a pick

In this chapter, we'll look at the different ways you can hold the uke, as well as basic playing technique.

HOLDING THE UKULELE

There are several different ways to hold the uke, and it's really a matter of personal preference as to which you choose.

Traditional Method

The most traditional way involves pressing it against your chest or rib cage with the right forearm. This will support most of the weight of the ukulele. Your left hand then provides the rest of the stability necessary so it doesn't fall. This position can be done sitting or standing.

It'll take a little bit of adjustment and practice to find the best position for you, so experiment until you find something that's comfortable.

try this

Here's a nifty trick for quickly getting the uke in position with this bracing method: Set the uke in front of you on a table or your lap with the headstock pointing left (reverse these directions if you're using a left-handed uke). Now grab the uke with your right hand by cradling the neck/body joint, extending your index finger along the fretboard. Once you have a good grip on it, simply bring it up to your chest and apply pressure with your forearm. That should get you in a good starting position.

Alternative Seated Method

Some people, when seated, prefer to rest the uke on their leg instead of cradling it with the forearm. This usually results in the uke being more angled, but many find this more comfortable.

Using a Strap

Many uke players prefer to use a strap instead of cradling it with the forearm, especially when standing. Aside from the added comfort some feel with this method, it can also change the sound of the uke a bit because the body is allowed to vibrate a bit more freely. This can sometimes result in a slightly fuller sound with more bass response.

You can use a standard guitar strap for this, assuming it's adjustable down to at least 40 inches or so.

There are also straps that are specifically designed for ukuleles that you wear more like a necklace and don't require any modification to your uke in the way of added strap buttons. These are another option to consider, especially if you don't like the idea of drilling into your instrument (although there's nothing to be afraid of—just ask any steel-string acoustic guitar!).

Most ukes don't come with strap buttons (though some do), but it's an easy matter to attach them. You can buy a pair for a few dollars, and if you're handy with a drill, you can install them in less than five minutes. You'll want to put one on the end that's opposite the headstock. The other side of the strap can be attached two different ways: You can either install a second strap button on the heel of the neck (as is the case with most acoustic guitars), or you can use a string to tie it around the headstock (the string would go under the strings, just behind the nut). Some straps are specifically designed for this application and feature a clip on one end that secures to the headstock.

RIGHT-HAND POSITION

Strumming

There are no hard-and-fast rules for strumming the uke. Many players use different methods—often times within the same song—to achieve great results. We'll look at the most common method here and then mention several variations with which you can experiment, as well.

As opposed to a guitar, where most players strum over the soundhole, the uke is usually strummed near the intersection of the neck and body—if not over the end of the neck itself. This generally produces what most people think of as the classic ukulele strum.

The typical method of strumming the uke involves using your index finger in a slightly curled position, with the other fingers tucked into a very loose fist. The strumming motion then comes from the wrist. Try to keep the motion light and fluid so that the index finger glides through the strings.

Listen to the audio to hear the sound of the index finger strumming the open strings, first using downstrokes and then with upstrokes. Then practice doing the same thing.

Strumming open strings with the index finger

Alternatively, you can strum with the thumb, using the same wrist motion. This produces a slightly different sound than the index finger. You can experiment with both to see which you prefer. Many players will use both methods, depending on the song. Listen to hear the same downstrokes and upstrokes on open strings, but this time with the thumb.

Strumming open strings with the thumb

Fingerpicking

You can also pluck individual notes (or the notes of chords) with your fingers instead of strumming through all the strings. Again, multiple methods are used in this regard. It's very common, however, for people to make use of their thumb, index, and middle fingers when fingerpicking. Some people prefer to use their ring finger, as well.

Practice planting your right-hand fingers on the strings as shown in the photos, plucking the strings individually to get a feel for it. Then try plucking all four strings simultaneously or in groups of three strings (4–3–2 or 3–2–1), concentrating on making sure each string is clearly heard.

Fingerpicking greatly expands the sonic possibilities of the uke, so I definitely recommend giving it a shot! You can find much more on the subject in Chapter 11.

LEFT-HAND POSITION

The other half of the equation is your left hand, which takes care of fretting the different notes. It's important in the early stages to develop a good fretting technique, as this will not only result in better tone, but it will also make your playing sound cleaner and more precise.

Basic Position

To get into a good starting position for your fretting hand, begin by holding the uke in playing position (with or without a strap). Drop your left arm to your side and then bring your hand up to gently hold the neck near the nut. Your fingers, slightly arched, should be contacting the strings and your thumb should be making contact on the back of the neck, near the middle, with its joint slightly extended back. Think about making a thumb print on a piece of paper, but then relax that extension a bit. Depending on the size and shape of your hand, the thumb should be roughly opposite your index finger. You want to find a natural position in which you're not straining the thumb in one direction or the other. Your wrist should be slightly flexed, which will allow you to arch the fingers more easily when fretting.

don't forget

- Keep your thumb roughly perpendicular to the neck.
- The palm should not be contacting the neck at all.
- Keep your fingers arched.
- The wrist should be slightly flexed

Remember that these are basic guidelines and there are occasional exceptions. Certain chords, for example, may require you to drop your thumb a bit lower than normal. Other times, as with barre chords, you'll be required to lay a finger flat across several strings.

Fretting Notes

When we fret a note, we push down on the string so that it makes full contact with the metal fret. This essentially changes the length of the string (the nut is basically acting like a "zero fret" when a string is played open) and therefore changes its pitch. The higher you fret up the string, the higher the pitch rises. You should make contact with the string just behind the fret wire—not directly on top of it and not too far back from it. Use the tips of your fingers and keep your fingers arched so that they don't prevent other strings from ringing clearly. The thumb presses against the back of the neck for added leverage.

Press down just behind the fret wire. If you're too close to the fret or too far back from it, you'll get a buzzy sound. For example, to play the note at fret 3 on string 2, press the string down between frets 2 and 3, but closer to fret 3. If you're still not getting a clear sound, make sure that you're pressing the string completely down to the fret and that your other fingers aren't making contact with the string in front of the fretting finger (i.e., between the fretting finger and the bridge). It's OK to make contact with the string behind the fretting finger (between the fretting finger and the nut).

If you're still not able to get a clean sound after trying the above suggestions, check your fingernails! If they're too long, they can be quite troublesome for playing the uke. Here's a good rule of thumb when checking their length: If, when drumming your fingers on a table, you're making contact with your nails before your fingertips, then the nails are most likely too long.

- Although guitarists usually strum with a pick, the ukulele is usually strummed with the index finger or the thumb.
- The uke can be played with or without a strap while standing or sitting, and there are several types of straps available.
- When you hear the term "fret" with regard to playing directions (as in "play the second fret"), this refers to the area in between the frets where you place your finger—not the fret wire itself.
- Remember that the strumming motion comes from the wrist; try to keep your right arm and wrist relaxed.
- On the left hand, keep your thumb behind the neck, opposite the index and/or middle finger. Keep the fingers arched when fretting.

CHAPTER 4
THE ART OF PRACTICE

> **What's Ahead:**
> * How to practice
> * What to practice
> * How to warm up
> * Creating and maintaining a practice schedule
> * How to practice away from the ukulele

Everyone knows that practice is the only way to get better at something. The more you practice, the better you'll get. Seems simple, right? But it's not always that easy. Sometimes knowing what to practice is trickier than it seems. And making the most of your practice time is certainly not as easy as it sounds. You can significantly speed up your improvement on the ukulele by taking control of your practice time and making it work for you. In this chapter, we'll look at this all-important but often-neglected topic.

PREPARATION
Before you can have a productive practice session, there are some essentials that need to be addressed, namely:

1. Practice time
2. Practice space
3. Practice materials

Practice Time
If you can set a time every day to practice and stick to it, that's ideal. Of course, that's not an option for everyone, and that's OK. As long as you're structured with the time you have, you're going to see great results. It's fun to play the ukulele, and therefore it's easy to blow through a whole hour doing nothing but "playing" instead of practicing. And that's fine to do on occasion. But if you want to progress on the instrument, you don't want that to be the norm. A structured, deliberate approach will yield better results. Making a list of what you'd like to work on for each session can be very helpful in this regard.

Practice Space
You also need a place to practice, and it's important to find somewhere that's comfortable and free from distractions. If you're using your phone as a timer, be sure to turn off the ringer and other notifications so that you're not distracted by those things. Also, be mindful of your posture—don't slump or slouch—as this can help you avoid getting a sore back or neck when playing for an extended period of time. You'll also want to make sure your space has plenty of light (for reading your music) and, of course, a comfortable temperature.

Practice Materials
Be sure you have everything you need in your practice space before you start your session. This not only includes any musical materials you're going to be working on (sheet music, books, videos, etc.), but also other helpful equipment such as a metronome, recorder, CD/MP3 player, pens/pencils, blank staff paper, tuner, etc. It's very frustrating to get situated and start practicing only to realize that you have to get up for something in the middle of it.

PRACTICE SCHEDULE

How Much Time Should I Spend Practicing?

The amount of time you spend practicing will depend on many factors, including your current schedule, your musical goals, and your personality, among others. Do you mainly want to just strum the uke and sing songs around a campfire? Or do you want to shred like Jake Shimabukuro? Obviously, the latter will require much more work!

As a general guideline, 30–60 minutes per day is appropriate for a beginner. Just about everyone can squeeze an extra 30 minutes out of their day for something that's important to them. If you can't do it every day, that's OK. But you do want to try to practice as regularly as possible. You'll get much more benefit from practicing 30 minutes five or six days out of the week than you will if you play for three hours only on a Saturday, for example.

try this

> Recent studies have suggested that it's more effective to *recall* a skill during the same practice routine than to only work on it once. In other words, let's say you have an hour to practice and you want to work on learning new chords, strumming, and fingerpicking. Rather than practice new chords for 20 minutes, strumming for 20 minutes, and fingerpicking for 20 minutes, it's actually more effective to practice each for 10 minutes and then repeat that cycle.
>
> However you decide to divide up your routine, make sure to use a timer (your phone most likely has one) to keep you on track!

What Should I Practice?

This is another topic that will vary from person to person, as it depends largely on what you'd like to accomplish with the instrument. Nevertheless, I'd recommend that you start off with a fairly well-rounded approach to the instrument. Not only will this make you a more accomplished player, but it will also reveal to you which areas of study are most interesting, thereby allowing you to customize your routine.

Generally speaking, a typical practice session will include the following basic topics:

- Warming up
- Technique exercises
- Repertoire (established or new)

Warming Up

Although playing the uke may not be as physically demanding as competing in a triathlon, it nevertheless uses very specific muscles in very specific ways. Believe it or not, it's quite possible to suffer injury if you place too much strain on these muscles by implementing poor habits. Granted, if you're someone who just picks up the uke and strums a few songs once a week or so, the chances of injury are incredibly small. But if you make it a habit of practicing for long stretches (several hours) every day and don't bother to warm up properly, you could be asking for trouble.

Warming up gets the blood flowing through your hands and arms and prepares your body for the task at hand. Several exercises can be done in this regard:

- Repeatedly clenching and releasing a fist for a minute

- Extending a hand out (as if making a "stop" gesture) and gently pulling the fingertips toward yourself with your other hand—"gently" being the key word! It should feel like a stretch and not severe pain!

- Clasping your hands and reaching above your head as far as you can (this is good for the arms and back)

- Clasping your hands and reaching behind your back as far as you can, trying to create a 90-degree angle between your arms and back (also good for the arms and back)
- Making the "prayer" gesture and then applying pressure to stretch the forearms and wrists.
- Performing "windmills" (while standing, swing each arm in a wide circle as if imitating a free stroke in swimming)

These exercises will greatly help to get your body primed for a practice session. After that's done, it's also helpful to briefly warm up on the ukulele before beginning your official practice routine. There's no set method here, but the recommendation is to simply start off slowly and deliberately. Perhaps strum a few chords or play a few scales, slowly and evenly. The point is to be very controlled and deliberate in your execution here, as this will help set a precedent for the remainder of your session.

Please heed these warnings and make warming up part of your daily routine. Generally speaking, you needn't spend more than three or four minutes on it, but the benefits are great. Tendonitis and Carpal Tunnel Syndrome are no laughing matter!

Technique Exercises

This is a wide-ranging topic that can include anything from running scales to practicing finger-picking patterns. These exercises aren't always the most musical things in the world, but they're critical in developing your fine motor skills, which will enable you to actually make real-world music when called upon. Exercises should focus on both hands—fretting and plucking/strumming—and stress accuracy. It's better to play something slowly but cleanly rather than fast but sloppy. Typical topics will include scales and sequences, strumming patterns, fingerpicking patterns, legato techniques (hammer-ons, pull-offs, etc.), and chord voicings, among others.

Repertoire

Your repertoire is basically the list of songs or pieces that you have under your belt. Learning songs—complete songs—is more beneficial than many people know. Besides the fact that it will make you more fun at campfires, you'll most likely learn quite a bit during the process of learning a new song. It may contain a new chord progression that you've never seen, or the melody may be based off a new scale you've not encountered before. Perhaps the strum pattern will be new to you, or maybe the time signature is not something you normally play in. Learning a song from front to back will help your memorization skills, as well.

A *chord* is a group of three or more notes played simultaneously in a harmonious fashion. As you will discover throughout this book, there are many different types of chords, and they all sound unique. Songs are usually made up of *chord progressions*, which is a term denoting several chords strung together into a repetitive pattern.

A *scale* is a collection of notes used to play melodies or chords in a song. Oftentimes, especially in pop music, the same scale is used for both the chords and the melodies for the whole song. In other types of music, such as jazz and classical, many different scales can be used within the same piece. Most scales contain seven different notes, with its first note regarded as the *tonic*, or *root*. The note from which a chord gets its name is also called the *root* of the chord. For example, in a C chord, the root of the chord is C.

When learning a song, get rid of the chart as soon as possible! After reading through the song with the chart once or twice, immediately get rid of it and start trying to play the song by memory. From that point on, only reference the chart when you absolutely need to, and only for the specific parts needed. The sooner you force yourself to use your memory, the sooner you will commit the song to memory.

SETTING GOALS

Something that many musicians face in their musical development are plateaus. These are times when it seems as though you're just treading water and not really making progress. Plateaus can be extremely frustrating and can even cause some people to abandon an instrument altogether. Fortunately, there's a good way to avoid them, and that is the act of setting goals for yourself. What many people don't realize is that a plateau is often self-inflicted because they've simply lost focus in their practice sessions and ended up just playing things they already know.

When you set goals for yourself, you give yourself that all-important focus. When you know where you want to go, it's much easier to get there. Therefore, you should make it a habit of regularly assessing your progress and listing new goals for yourself. It could be something you do every week or perhaps every month, depending on the amount of time you have to practice.

For example, you may say, "OK, by the end of this week, I'd like to have this list of chords under my fingers and be able to play these scales at this tempo." You can get incredibly specific or remain a bit looser with it ("I want to learn to play two different songs this week"), but the act of setting your sights on something and then working towards it is crucial to your progress. The good news is that I can guarantee you're never going to run out of goals to achieve!

REMOTE PRACTICING (WHEN YOU DON'T HAVE A UKE IN HAND)

It may seem like a far-fetched idea, but there will be times when you actually don't have your ukulele within plucking distance! Never fear—you can still improve as a musician! Here are several tricks that will pay dividends even when the closest uke is one county away:

* Use your right-hand forearm as a uke neck and practice fingering your chords and scales. Imagine the four strings and the fret wire and create the appropriate shapes with your left hand. (Whether or not you want to draw a uke neck on your arm is up to you.)
* With your hands on a table, practice drumming your left-hand fingers in various orders. For example, try index-middle-ring-pinky or reverse that. Try index-ring-middle-pinky (or the reverse) or index-pinky-middle-ring, etc. This is great for developing finger independence.
* While listening to a song (on headphones or a stereo, etc.), try to strum along to the rhythmic pattern—air guitar-style—while tapping your foot to the beat.

Developing Your Ear

And there's plenty you can do that's not specifically ukulele-related, as well. It's also very important to develop your ear as a musician. You may have seen or heard someone that can, after only hearing a song one time, immediately play the song on their instrument without any practice. This obviously takes something in the way of physical skill, but mostly it takes a good ear. This means the ability to distinguish notes/chords/melodies simply by hearing them. You don't have to have *perfect pitch* (the ability to recognize any note just by listening to it) to do this; you only need a well-developed sense of *relative pitch*. This refers to the ability to identify musical *intervals* (the musical distance between notes) and other note/chord relationships.

For example, a person with perfect pitch can hear the note G on a piano without looking and identify it as a G note. Someone with relative pitch can't do this. However, if they first hear a C note, for example, and the pianist tells them it's a C note, then someone with good relative pitch could easily recognize a subsequent G note, A note, B♭ note, or any other note. They just need a framework with which to start.

More importantly, though, they're able to recognize musical materials so that, when they get to their instrument, they can quickly reproduce them once they've established the pitch. For example, they may hear a melody and immediately know it's from the major scale, even though they don't know which major scale it's from. Or they may hear a chord progression and know the quality of every chord without knowing the specific pitch level. However, upon plucking a few notes on the uke to get their bearings, they will immediately be able to play the chord progression or the scale they heard.

Here are some ways to work on this skill:

- Make it a habit of closely listening to music whenever present. This means listening with intent. Try to listen to the chords and notice patterns that repeat. Try to identify which note feels like "home" or feels the most resolved; this note is likely the key of the song. Pay attention to any chords that stick out from the rest and try to identify which note(s) in the chord is sticking out specifically.

- When you hear a melody (sung or played by an instrument), try to imagine playing the melody on your ukulele. Visualize what frets and strings would contain those notes. Once you have a uke in hand again, check your work to see if you were right. Obviously, the more you do this, the better you'll become, but you'd be surprised how quickly you can start getting things right.

- Practice singing or humming a melody and then playing it back on the uke. You may have to hunt and peck a bit at first, but you'll eventually begin to recognize which fretboard shapes will produce which sounds.

- Try to practice for 30–60 minutes every day, if possible.

- Focused, deliberate practice will yield better results than aimless noodling.

- Warm up before each practice session.

- Remember to practice away from the ukulele when possible.

- Building a repertoire of songs is beneficial in more ways than one.

The Basics of Playing

CHAPTER 5

MUSIC NOTATION FOR UKULELE

What's Ahead:
- Chord grids
- Ukulele tablature
- Box scale frames
- A closer look at a chord

All right, now it's time to start getting down to business. In this chapter, we're going to look at some popular forms of notation for the ukulele, which we'll be using throughout the rest of this book when we learn to play chords, melodies, and so on.

CHORD GRIDS

Chord grids (also called *chord frames* or *chord diagrams*), are a quick and convenient way to notate how a chord is to be played on the ukulele. Oftentimes, you'll see these above the *chord symbols* (the chord "names" that appears above the notes on a musical staff) in ukulele or guitar music. You can kind of think of them as the "CliffsNotes" of notation. They tell you the essentials (i.e., what notes are in the chord and how it's fingered), but they don't communicate anything with regard to the rhythm in which they're played. For that, we need a bit more detailed notation, which we'll look at in a subsequent chapter. But for singing songs around a campfire, they're usually more than adequate.

Basically, a chord grid is a visual representation of the ukulele fretboard. They're usually drawn vertically, as if you had stood the uke on end (with the headstock pointed to the ceiling) and turned it so that the neck is facing you.

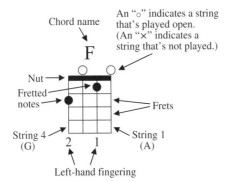

An "o" indicates a string that's played open. (An "×" indicates a string that's not played.)

Chord name

F

Nut
Fretted notes
Frets
String 4 (G)
String 1 (A)
2   1
Left-hand fingering

- The four vertical lines represent the strings, progressing from string 4 (on the left) to string 1 (on the right).
- The thick horizontal line at the top represents the nut.
- The thin horizontal lines represent the frets.
- An "O" above a string indicates that it's to be played open (unfretted).
- An "X" will appear above a string when it's not to be played at all.
- Dots are used to show fretted notes.
- The numbers along the bottom indicate the suggested left-hand fingering, with "1" representing the index finger, "2" representing the middle finger, and so on.

Sometimes a chord is not played in open position (i.e., it's played farther up the neck). In those instances, a fret number indicates the starting fret, or the lowest fret in the grid.

UKULELE TABLATURE

Tablature (or *tab* for short) is an easy way to get a bit more specific with ukulele notation. It allows you to write specific notes on a staff that represent distinct pitches. It's still a visual representation, but in a different way. Here's how it looks:

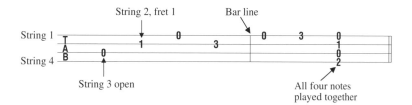

- The word "tab" at the beginning of the staff lets you know this is a tablature staff.
- Similar to a chord grid, there are four lines representing the strings. In tab, however, these lines are horizontal, as with a normal music staff. String 4 is on the bottom, and string 1 is on the top.
- The numbers on the lines represent the frets or open strings to be played. In the example above, the open third string is played first, then the first fret on the second string is played, followed by the open first string, and so on.
- When several numbers are stacked, those are to be played together as a chord.
- The vertical lines are *bar lines* and have nothing to do with the fretboard. They break the music up into measures (which we'll look at in a bit), the same as with standard notation.

Tab can be a little confusing at first, especially when coming from chord grids, which are orientated vertically. To help visualize the neck in tab form, lay the ukulele on your lap, face up, with the headstock pointed left. This is the view of the neck when looking at a tab staff. It's essentially orientated the way the neck appears when you look down at it from playing position.

BOX SCALE FRAMES

The *box frame* (also called a *scale diagram* or *fretboard diagram*) is very similar to the chord grid, but it's used to indicate scale forms on the neck. However, whereas chord grids are orientated vertically, box scale frames are usually orientated horizontally, similar to the tab staff. Occasionally, you will see them turned on end vertically like a chord grid, but more often than not, they're horizontal. Either way, they operate the same; one is just rotated 90 degrees from the other.

- The horizontal lines represent the strings, with string 4 on the bottom and string 1 on the top.
- The vertical lines represent the frets. The thick line on the left represents the nut.
- Dots are used to show fretted notes; an "O" is used to show a string played open. (As opposed to a chord grid, an "X" usually doesn't appear next to an unused string in a scale frame.)
- The tonic note of the scale (the note from which the scale gets its name) is often circled or delineated in some other way (perhaps appearing as a hollow circle instead of a solid dot).

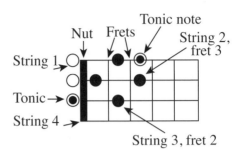

Essentially, scale frames are used to show a collection of notes (usually a scale). Unlike a chord, however, these notes are not meant to be played simultaneously (that would be impossible). Rather, they're meant to be played one at a time from low to high or from high to low.

Just as with a chord grid, a scale frame can appear further up the neck. In those instances, there will be a thin line at the left, and a fret number will indicate the lowest fret in the frame.

CHORDS: A CLOSER LOOK

Generally speaking, a chord is made up of three or more notes played (or at least fingered) simultaneously. The *chord voicing* is the specific arrangement of these notes on the ukulele fretboard. There are many ways to play the same chord on the uke. The F chord that appeared at the beginning of this chapter was voiced in what's called "open position," because it appeared within the first few frets and made use of both open strings and fretted notes. The Gm chord (which stands for "G minor") is in "fifth position" because the lowest fret used in the chord is fret 5.

The most common chord in music is the major chord, which contains three specific notes. For example, the F major chord contains the notes F, A, and C. To play this on the uke, we play all three of these notes simultaneously. If you happened to notice that there were four notes in our F chord, don't worry; this is not a mistake. There are four notes, but there are only three *different* pitches. One of the notes (an A note in this case) is doubled. In other words, the note on string 4 sounds exactly the same as the one on string 1. Doubling a note this way is very common in ukulele chords, although there are other types of chords that contain four unique notes (we'll look at them a bit later).

A chord with three different notes is called a *triad*. The two most common types of triads are *major* and *minor*. A chord symbol with only a capital letter represents a major triad; for minor chords, we add an "m" to the chord symbol. In other words, the chord symbol "C" indicates a C major triad, whereas the chord symbol "Cm" indicates a C minor triad.

The terms "triad" and "chord" can often be used interchangeably and share the same relationship as a square and a rectangle. In other words, all squares are rectangles, but not all rectangles are squares. In the same way, all triads are chords, but not all chords are triads. A triad is simply one type of chord.

CHAPTER 6
BASIC CHORDS

What's Ahead:
- Your first chord
- Open-position major and minor chords
- Chord "families"
- Common chord progressions
- Strumming patterns
- Play-along songs

It's time to learn how to do what the ukulele does best: play chords. There's nothing like the sound of someone strummin' the uke. That light, buoyant sound can put a smile on just about anyone's face. Armed with a handful of chords and a uke, you've got one of the most portable jukeboxes on the planet. Just add some vocals (either your own or someone else's), and you've got all you need to pass the time.

Over the past decade, the uke has experienced a remarkable resurgence, and you can hear it cropping up in all kinds of pop songs, from Train's "Hey, Soul Sister" and Vance Joy's "Riptide" to Eddie Vedder's *Ukulele Songs* album, the instrument is riding the airwaves more and more all the time. In just about all of these instances, the artists are just strummin' the uke!

YOUR FIRST CHORD

Let's get down to it and learn your first chord. As mentioned earlier, a chord is made up of three or more notes played simultaneously. Of course, you don't just pick three random notes; the results will likely not be too musically pleasing. We use specifically grouped sets of notes that are arranged into chord shapes. These are both (usually) easy to play and sound great.

Whereas chords are usually strummed with a pick on a guitar, on the uke, we usually forego the pick and just strum them with the index finger or thumb. Most ukulele chords involve all four strings, which makes it easier on the strumming hand because we don't have to worry about only hitting certain strings. The most common chords on the uke are the open-position variety, which, as mentioned before, contain a mix of open strings and fretted notes.

The C Major Chord

For our first chord, we're going to look at C major, also known simply as a C chord.

A chord symbol consisting of just a capital letter indicates a major chord. So, "C" indicates a C major chord; "G" indicates a G major chord, etc.

Take a look at the chord grid to make sense of the C chord. This is one of the easiest chords to play on the uke because we only need to fret one note. Most chords will require you to use more than one finger, but we luck out with the C chord.

Notice that there's a "3" at the bottom of the grid, below string 1. This tells you to use your ring finger for that note. Place it there now. Remember that you should press the string down slightly behind the third fret—not on top of it and not too far back. Use enough pressure to make a solid connection to the fretboard, but there's no need to press down so hard that your finger tip turns white or anything. (Pressing down too hard can actually make the string go out of tune!)

Once you have your third finger in place on the first string at the third fret, use your right-hand thumb to brush through all the strings in a downward motion toward the floor. And there you have it! You just played your first C chord!

Something's Wrong: Troubleshooting Your First Chord

It's not uncommon for your first effort to sound less than glorious. Don't worry—it happens to most of us. Here's a checklist to look over (with any chord) before you return your ukulele to the store and tell them it's broken:

* **Are you in tune?** This is by far the most common issue with beginners. Keep in mind that it's not uncommon for new ukulele strings to stretch for the first day or two after being put on. So, be sure to check the tuning again with a tuner, especially if you have new strings on your uke.

* **Are you pushing the string(s) down hard enough?** If you're not applying enough pressure, the string won't make solid contact with the fret wire and will result in a buzzing tone. When you first start playing, your fingertips will likely get a bit sore (see "Developing Calluses" sidebar) after playing. This is perfectly normal and will pass in time. Just take a break when you need to.

* **Are you bending a string accidentally?** When you push a string up (toward the ceiling) or down (toward the floor), you're *bending* the string. Bending a string up or down will cause the string to go sharp (because you're increasing the string's tension). Make sure you're not accidentally pushing one of the strings out of alignment.

* **Are you accidentally muting strings?** This is another very common mistake that beginners make, especially if you have large hands. You'll want to make sure that a fretting finger isn't accidentally making contact with an adjacent string, as this will mute that string (i.e., stop it from ringing). In our C chord, for example, make sure that you're not touching string 2 with your third finger while fretting string 1.

Developing Calluses

If you've ever known a player of a stringed instrument (guitar, bass, violin, cello, etc.), you may have noticed that they have hard fingertips on their fretting hand. This is because, as you play more and more, you'll build up calluses on your fingertips. This is a good thing! It means that you won't get sore from playing like you did when just starting out. It doesn't take too long to build up a good set of calluses—anywhere from a few weeks to a month or so, depending on how frequently you play. Once you've played through the chords in this chapter several times, you'll probably already start noticing a difference. Until then, though, remember that this is not the Marine Corps. There's no need to play through the pain, so take a break when you need to!

OPEN-POSITION MAJOR AND MINOR CHORDS

You don't need to know a lot of uke chords to play a lot of songs. In fact, you can play hundreds of songs by learning a handful of chords in open position. As mentioned earlier, an open-position chord is one that's played near the nut and mixes open strings with fretted notes. You already learned your first one, C major, so now we'll add to your chord vocabulary.

Every song is in what's called a "key." The key of a song is based on the note that feels like "home." Therefore, it's often the final note of a vocal melody in a song. Take "Star Spangled Banner," for example. The final line of the song goes, "and the home of the **brave**." The note on the word "brave" is also the key of the song. It feels resolved when you hear it. Imagine if someone sang, "and the home of the…" and then stopped. You wouldn't be able to move on with your day until hearing the completion of that melody! This helps to illustrate how powerful the key of a piece really is.

With regard to chords, each key has its own *chord family*, which is a set of chords that are commonly used in that key. While it's true that you can use any chord in a song—there aren't any "laws" in music preventing you from doing that—history has shown us that certain chords sound really good together, and therefore people tend to use them often. By learning chord families in several common uke keys, you'll be able to play hundreds of songs.

F Major and G Major

Two other chords that sound great with a C major chord are G major and F major. Both of these chords belong to the C chord family and therefore are often found in songs that are in the key of C major. Using the following chord grids and pictures, let's learn how to play these two chords now.

For the F chord (remember: If given no other information, a capital-letter chord name implies a major chord), you'll fret two notes. Place your first finger on fret 1 of string 2 and then add your second finger to fret 2 of string 4. In this case, your first finger has adjacent strings on both sides of it, so it's very important to fret with the tip of the finger and keep it arched so that you're not accidentally touching string 1 or string 3. Also be sure not to touch string 3 with your middle finger while fretting string 4.

Notice in the photo that the thumb is kept behind the neck. Also notice that, again, the fingers are placed just behind the fret to produce a clear sound. Once you have the fingers in position, brush through the strings with your thumb.

G

1 3 2

The G chord requires three fingers to play. Begin by placing your first finger at fret 2 on string 3. Next, add your third finger at fret 3 on string 2. Finally, add your second finger at fret 2 on string 1. Notice the triangle shape that's made with this chord; this can be a handy aid in remembering it. Once all fingers are in place, brush through the strings to play the chord.

Changing Chords

Now that you've learned a few chords, let's work on the all-important concept of switching between them. This is a crucial skill that, when performed well, can really give your uke playing a professional sound. The idea here is that you want to minimize the gap that occurs in between chords.

To get started, let's try switching between C and F chords. Just strum each one slowly four times and go back and forth between the two. Listen to the audio to hear how this should sound.

Switching between C and F chords

Notating Simple Chord Strums

As a quick detour, let's take a look at how we can notate what you just played. For this, we'll use a standard notation staff with a *treble clef*, but we're still not going to be using any notes on the staff. Instead, we'll use a shorthand called *rhythm slashes*. These are simply dash marks indicating a chord strum.

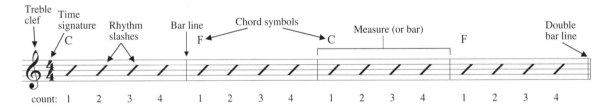

We won't get too deep into music theory just yet, but let's take a quick moment to discuss the various symbols used here:

- The *musical staff* consists of five horizontal lines and four spaces, each of which represents a note. Music is read left to right on the staff, just like words in a book.

- The *treble clef* tells you which type of staff is being used. Most instruments, including the uke, read treble clef, but some instruments use other clefs. For example, bass instruments, like a bass guitar, read bass clef.

- The *time signature* tells you how the song is counted. The most common signature is 4/4, which tells you there are four beats in each *measure*, or *bar*, of music.

- *Bar lines* separate the music into measures. You can kind of think of them as punctuation marks in a book. It would be very hard to keep your place in a book if the text wasn't broken up into sentences and paragraphs. A *double bar line* often appears at the end of a section or at the end of an example.

- The *chord symbols* appear above the staff, and the *rhythm slashes* indicate when you should strum. In the above example, you're strumming once on every beat (i.e., four times in every measure).

Now let's try moving between C and G chords. Just as before, strum four times in each measure.

Keep the following tips in mind when changing from chord to chord.

- **Only move a finger if and when necessary:** When moving from C to F, for example, you start with your ring finger on string 1 at fret 3 for the C chord. For the F chord, you use your middle and index fingers on strings 4 and 2 at frets 2 and 1, respectively. Therefore, you can keep your third finger down right up until the very end.

- **Visualize the next chord in your mind before playing it:** This helps in preparing to set your fingers in action when the time comes.

- **If any open strings are used in both chords, make every attempt to keep them ringing through both chords:** When moving from C to F, the open third string (C) appears in both chords, so be sure to keep it ringing when making the change. Likewise, when moving from C to G, the open fourth string (G) is used for both chords.

- **Don't be afraid to use alternate fingerings for chords if it makes it easier:** When moving from C to G, you have to lift your third finger off string 1 (used for the C chord) and move it to string 2 for the G chord (while adding the first and second fingers as well). However, there's no law that says you *have* to use the ring finger for the C chord. In this instance, it's easier to use the pinky for the C chord and then use the other three fingers for the G chord!

D Major and A Major

Let's learn two more major chords now: D and A. Taken together with our G chord, these belong to the D major family (i.e., the key of D major).

The D chord is the trickiest one yet because it requires you to squeeze three fingers into one fret. And, as you may have noticed, the frets on the uke aren't all that big! For people with big hands, this one can be really tough. (There are alternatives, which we'll look at a bit later!) We're listing three possible fingerings for this chord because people use them all. If you use the top-row fingering, you'll notice that it's very easy to go between D and A chords, which is a benefit because that's a common chord move.

A major is much easier and only requires two fingers. Place your middle finger on fret 2 of string 4 and your index finger on fret 1 of string 3. Strings 2 and 1 are open.

Try moving back and forth between the D and A chords. Notice the benefit of using the top-row fingering for D major when doing this; you don't have to move your middle finger at all!

When two chords share a note, it's called a *common tone*. We already saw this with the C and F chords, which both contain the open third string (C). Our D and A chords have a common tone as well; in fact, they have two: fret 2 on string 4 and the open first string. Coincidentally, both of these are the same A note.

Whenever two chords have a common tone, it will sound smoother if you can figure out a way to fret them so that one finger can remain in place for both chords. It's not crucial, but it's certainly nice to do when possible.

Playing Your First Songs—Key of D Major

We only need our D and A chords to play the fun children's song "Skip to My Lou." On the following page, you'll see the song notated with two staves: one for the vocal melody and one for the uke rhythm slashes. Don't worry about reading the vocal melody yet; we'll get to that later on. For now, just work on strumming the chords in time, once per beat, and changing smoothly between them.

Once you have it down and can play along to the audio without stopping, try singing the song while you play. Even though the melody contains some faster notes, remember to strum just once per beat. You may be tempted to try and strum in the same rhythm that you're singing at first, but this will improve with practice. Tapping your foot with the beat should help in this regard. In the very last measure, strum three times, letting the last one ring for two counts.

Remember that, when the song is over, you need to stop the sound of your ukulele. To do this, simply touch the strings with your right hand to stop them from ringing.

Skip to My Lou

Traditional

audio
tracks
5

Fly's in the but-ter-milk; shoo fly, shoo! Fly's in the but-ter-milk; shoo fly, shoo!

Fly's in the but-ter-milk; shoo fly, shoo! Skip to my Lou, my dar - ling.

Skip, skip, skip to my Lou. Skip, skip, skip to my Lou.

Skip, skip, skip to my Lou. Skip to my Lou, my dar - ling.

(hold chord
2 counts)

try this

Try strumming with your thumb first, as we've been doing. Then try playing the example again, but this time using your index finger to strum. Each method has a different sound, and both are useful. The thumb has a nice, round sound that's really good for ballads and slow songs, whereas the index finger produces a lighter, more trebly sound that works well for quicker strums. You should try to become familiar with both techniques.

That was fun, right? So, let's do another one. If we add another chord to our D family, G major, we can play literally hundreds of three-chord songs. Let's try Bob Marley's "Stir It Up," which contains D, G, and A chords. Again, we'll strum once per beat, and remember to tap your foot as you play.

Stir It Up

Words and Music by Bob Marley

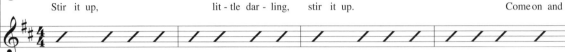

When you play several chords in a repeating pattern, it's called a *chord progression*. Many songs use the same chord progressions over and over, which you will no doubt recognize as you progress in your studies. We'll eventually look at how you can play the same progression in different keys (or different chord families). This is also extremely common in the music world.

It's helpful to realize, if you haven't already, that one chord can (and always does) belong to more than one chord family. In fact, we've already seen evidence of this with our G chord. If you remember, we first said it belonged to the C major chord family. But then we said it also belongs to the D major chord family. In fact, each chord family (i.e., each key) contains seven different chords.

Since there are 12 keys, and each contains seven chords in its family, then you can do the math and realize that some chords must be shared by several keys.

A Minor and D Minor Chords

Now it's time to learn our first minor chords. If you remember, a while back we said that major and minor are the two most common chords. The reason is that they have sort of a yin-and-yang relationship. While a major chord sounds bright or happy, a minor chord sounds dark or sad. Every chord family (or key) actually contains a mixture of major and minor chords. Although you don't need minor chords to write a song—as we said, you can play hundreds of songs with three major chords—many songs contain both types.

Am

The A minor chord, along with C major, is one of the easiest chords to play on the uke. Just place your middle finger on string 4 at fret 2, and you've got it. The other strings are played open.

don't forget

The chord symbol for a major chord is simply an uppercase letter; so, "A" stands for "A major." A minor chord requires a lowercase "m" after the letter; so, "Am" stands for "A minor."

Dm

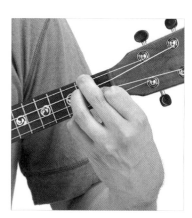

For D minor, you can keep your middle finger on fret 2, string 4 (where it was for A minor), then just add your ring finger to fret 2, string 3 and your index finger to fret 1, string 2. The first string is open.

Strumming Patterns

Since different songs have different rhythmic feels—the rhythm of Nirvana's "Teen Spirit" sounds very different from the Beatles' "Norwegian Wood," for example—we'll learn several different *strumming patterns* to help simulate the feel of different songs. In order to do this, we need to learn just a little bit about rhythmic notation. Check out the example below.

Notice that it's just like our previous examples, with one exception: we've added a *stem* (vertical line) to each rhythmic slash. This turns the slashes into quarter notes. Nevertheless, the two will sound exactly the same because quarter notes are counted as one beat. In other words, a measure in 4/4 time has four quarter notes in it.

If you were really on your game, you may have noticed that we snuck a bit of this into "Skip to My Lou." The last strum of the song had a stem with a hollow slash. This was a *half note*, which receives two beats. So, if a quarter note receives one beat, and a half note receives two beats, can you guess what a *whole note* receives? If you said four beats, you're right! Let's take a look at them systematically.

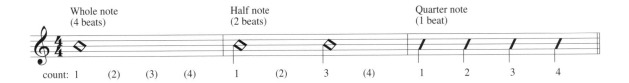

For our new strumming pattern, we're going to learn one more subdivision, which is the *eighth note*. The eighth note simply divides things further. Thus, there are two eighth notes in the space of one quarter note (i.e., the eighth note receives half a beat). Here's our new strum pattern:

We have a few new elements here, so let's talk about them:

- Notice that we count eighth notes by inserting "and" in between our quarter-note counts. So, this pattern is counted: "one, two, three-and, four, one, two, three-and, four."

- The eighth notes are connected at the end of the stem by a *beam*. This is only the case when several of them appear together. When an eighth note appears by itself, it has a *flag:*

- The funny ⊓ and V symbols above the staff indicate downstrokes and upstrokes, respectively. We've been using all downstrokes thus far—one per beat. When strumming eighth notes, however, it's better to strum down on the beat and then strum up in between the beats, on the "and." In other words, if you're tapping your foot to the beat, you'd strum down when your foot is tapping on the floor and then up when your foot is off the ground.

Strumming up will feel (and sound) a little different than strumming down, so practice slowly alternating down- and up-strums to get the feel for it. Try to achieve a similar volume for each. They will sound slightly different from each other, and that's actually a good thing. But try to make sure one is not sticking out too much with regard to volume.

Songs in A Minor

Let's try this new strum pattern in a few songs that we'll play in the key of A minor. We'll use two more chords from the A minor family, F and G, to play the classic "All Along the Watchtower."

All Along the Watchtower

Words and Music by Bob Dylan

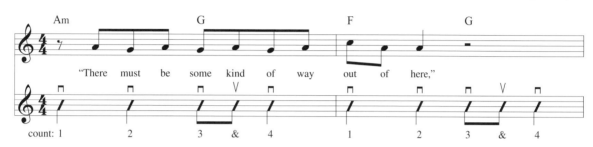

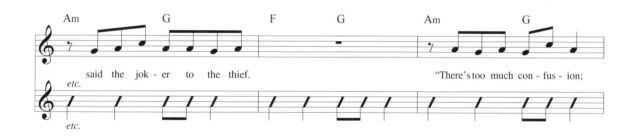

And now let's try to mix this new pattern with our original quarter-note strum in the Beatles' "Eleanor Rigby." We'll just be using Am and F chords here.

Notice the ‖: and :‖ symbols in the song. Those are called *repeat signs*, and they tell you to repeat the music that's enclosed within them.

Remember to watch for common tones between chords! Did you happen to notice that you can play "Eleanor Rigby" in its entirety without moving your left-hand middle finger at all?

B♭ Major, E♭ Major, and G Minor Chords

Let's add two more major chords and one more minor chord before we wrap up this chapter. B♭ (read: "B flat") and Gm are both in the F major chord family.

Gm

For the G minor chord, place your middle finger on fret 2, string 3. Then add your ring finger to fret 3, string 2 and your index finger to fret 1, string 1. The fourth string is open.

B♭

For the B♭ major chord, we'll be doing something we haven't done before. First, place your ring finger on fret 3 of string 4 and your middle finger on fret 2 of string 3. Now, lay your first finger across both strings 2 and 1 at fret 1. This means you'll be covering string 1 with the pad of your first finger rather than the tip. This technique—fretting adjacent strings with the same finger—is called *barring*. We'll look more closely at barres later on, but this is a good introduction to them, as it's only a partial barre (i.e., you're only barring two strings). Notice that a curved line is used to convey a barre on a chord grid.

Once you have everything in place, brush through the B♭ chord. Be sure to also pluck each string individually to make sure you're getting a clean sound.

The ♭ symbol is called a *flat*. You'll also see the *sharp* symbol ♯, another common symbol in music. Together, these are called *accidentals*, and they affect the notes to which they're attached.

It's easiest to understand sharps and flats if you look at a piano keyboard. All of the white keys are called *natural* notes, and the black keys are the accidentals. A sharp raises a note by one *half step* (the distance of one key—white or black—on the piano), whereas a flat lowers a note by one half step. So, for example, a G♯ note is the black key directly to the right of G (a white key) on the piano.

And, as another example, a B♭ note is the black key directly to the left of B (a white key) on the piano.

We'll talk a bit more about this later on.

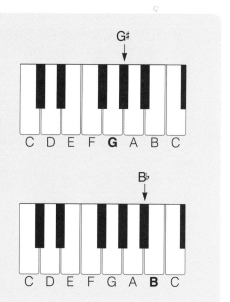

Eb

The Eb major chord is not too much trouble, but it's a good one with which to get some pinky practice. Place your ring finger on fret 3 of string 3, your pinky on fret 3 of string 2, and your index finger on fret 1 of string 1. The fourth string is played open.

Chord Progressions in F Major

Let's put our new Bb and Gm chords to use in a chord progression with F and C. This means our chord progression will have four different chords in it. We're also using our new strum pattern here. Remember to look for common tones between chords (hint: look at the Gm and Bb chords!).

The flat ♭ at the beginning of the previous example is called a *key signature*. A key signature indicates the key of a song and lets the performer know that certain notes should be played as flat or sharp throughout the piece. In this instance, it tells the performer to play Bb instead of B throughout. This avoids the need to write a flat in front of every B note. If you look back at pages 31 and 32, you'll also see a key signature used for the songs "Skip to My Lou" and "Stir It Up." That key signature, which contains two sharps, indicates the key of D major. All 12 major keys have their own key signature, as do all 12 minor keys. The key signature for C major and A minor is blank (i.e., there are no sharps or flats in those keys). Coincidentally, this means that if you play only the white keys on a piano, you'll always be playing notes in the key of C major (or A minor). Every other major or minor key will have a collection of sharps *or* flats in their key signature—never both.

Let's take another set of chords from the F chord family to play another progression. We'll be using F, C, Dm, and Am here with a new strumming pattern. This is just like our quarter-note strum pattern, but we're letting the second strum in each measure ring for a half note. So, instead of "strum–strum–strum–strum" for each measure, it's "strum–strum (let ring)–strum." Use all downstrokes for this pattern.

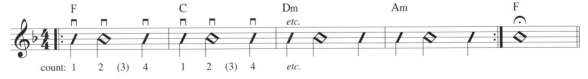

The ⌢ symbol that appears over the last chord in the previous example is called a *fermata*. It means that you should hold the chord for an extended, indefinite amount of time before stopping it.

CHORD FAMILY REVIEW

Let's take a second to review the chords we've learned thus far and see which chord families they fall into. Here are all the chords we've learned:

Major

C
F
G
D
A
B♭

Minor

Am
Dm
Gm

And now let's place them all into chord families.

Major Chord Families

C major: C, Dm, F, G, Am
F major: F, Gm, Am, B♭, C, Dm
G major: G, Am, C, D
D major: D, G, A
A major: A, D

Minor Chord Families

A minor: Am, C, Dm, F, G
D minor: Dm, F, Gm, Am, B♭, C
G minor: Gm, B♭, Dm, F

Keep in mind, this is not to say that these chord families are complete—for instance, there are more chords within the A major family than just A and D—but rather we're simply placing all the chords we've learned thus far into every possible chord family. And again, these chord families are not law; just because we didn't list Dm in the A major chord family doesn't mean you'll never hear a Dm chord in a song that's in A major (in fact, you certainly will if you listen to the Beatles at all!). But, in a strict sense, Dm is not part of the key of A major, so we didn't list it as such.

extras

The word we use to say something belongs to a key is *diatonic*. This can apply to notes or chords. So, for example, we may say that the note D is diatonic to the key of C major, but the note D♭ is non-diatonic. Or, we could say that a C major chord is diatonic to the key of F major, but an A major chord is non-diatonic.

Again, this doesn't mean that a D♭ note will never appear in a C major song or an A major chord will never appear in an F major song; it simply means that, when they do, it's not "business as usual," so to speak, and we'll have to use accidentals to notate them because they will use notes that are not within the key signature.

CHAPTER 7
SIMPLE SCALES AND MELODIES

What's Ahead:

- The music staff
- C major and F major scales
- Left-hand fingering
- Right-hand plucking
- Melodies in the keys of C major and F major
- D minor scale
- Melodies in the key of D minor

Now that you've got some chords under your belt, it's time to start tackling the other side of playing: melodies. Whereas chords consist of several notes played at once, melodies consist of several notes played in succession. As with chords, we'll make use of both fretted notes and open strings for melodies, but the coordination is a bit more exacting, especially with the plucking hand, as you'll need to pluck only one string at a time instead of strumming all four.

This will involve a bit more in the way of reading music, but the tab will be there to help you out, as will the audio tracks. We'll take it slowly, though, so don't worry—you won't need to become an ace sight-reader (someone who can read new music flawlessly at first sight) to get through this chapter!

THE MUSIC STAFF

Before we get going with scales, let's take a quick detour to get us up to speed on the music staff. Some of this may be a bit of a review, but it's necessary to get everyone up to speed before we move on.

The *staff* is constructed from five horizontal lines and four spaces (between the lines). Each line and space represents a note. Remember from earlier that we said there are different kinds of *clefs*, which assign different notes to the lines and spaces of the staff. The ukulele reads *treble clef*, which is the most common type of clef.

On the treble clef, the notes on the lines are, from low to high, E, G, B, D, and F. The notes on the spaces are, from low to high, F, A, C, and E.

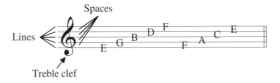

The spaces are easy to remember because they simply spell "**FACE**." To remember the notes on the lines, you can use "**E**very **G**ood **B**oy **D**oes **F**ine."

Notice that, when taken altogether, they simply ascend through the musical alphabet, which contains the letters A–G. When we reach G, we start over at A again in a higher *octave*. When we need to extend notes above or below the staff, we use *ledger lines*.

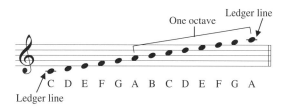

As we learned earlier, music is read from left to right on the staff and is divided into measures, or bars, by bar lines. A *double bar line* is often used at the end of an example or a section in a song, and a *terminal bar line*, or *end bar line*, appears at the end of a song.

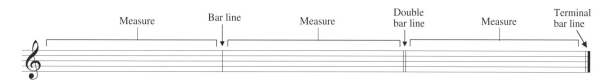

The *time signature* indicates the rhythm, or *meter*, of the music and consists of two stacked numbers. The top number indicates the number of beats in a measure, and the bottom number indicates which type of note is counted as one beat. Although we've only looked at 4/4 so far, there are several different common time signatures.

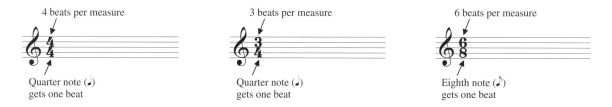

The rhythm (duration) of each note is indicated by its shape and appearance. We briefly looked at these earlier with rhythm slashes, but here's how they look with normal notes:

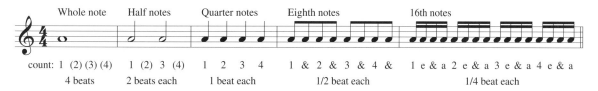

Since music also consists of silence, we need a way to notate that as well. We use different *rests* to indicate durations of silence.

YOUR FIRST SCALE

Before we can play our first melodies, we'll need to learn a scale with which to play them. The first scale we'll learn is the most ubiquitous of all, C major. In fact, if you simply drag your finger up or down just the white keys of a piano, you'd be playing the notes of the C major scale.

The C Major Scale

The major scale is the most common scale in music. It's the "do-re-mi" scale we all heard growing up. The major scale contains seven different notes, with the first note being the *tonic*. In the C major scale, C is the tonic; in the G major scale, G is the tonic, and so on.

The C major scale contains the following notes: C–D–E–F–G–A–B.

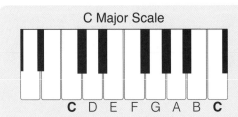

It's very easy to play the C major scale on a piano; just start at a C note ("middle C" is a good place to start) and then play every white key until you reach C again.

On a standard ukulele in reentrant tuning, C is actually the lowest pitched note we can play—the open third string—and that's where we'll start our C major scale. Here it is laid out all along the third string:

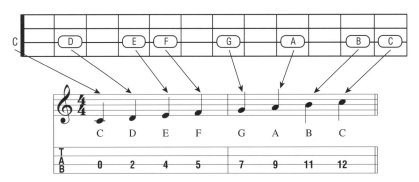

While this isn't the most practical way to play the scale, it's an excellent visual guide. Comparing this to the piano diagram in the previous **extras** sidebar is quite helpful. Notice that, when we have two white keys directly next to each other on the piano, we have two frets right next to each other on the ukulele. Specifically, this happens between E and F and between B and C.

If you refer back to page 6, you'll recall that the distance of one fret on the ukulele is the interval of a *half step*. This is the smallest musical interval (distance between notes) we have in Western music. This means that the musical alphabet has two natural half steps within it: from E to F and from B to C. If one fret represents a half step, can you guess what interval two frets represents? If you said a whole step, you're right! A *whole step* is twice that of a half step. On a piano keyboard, from C to D is a whole step because there's a black key in between them. The same is true for G to A and D to E.

Said in another way:

* A half step is the distance of one fret (along one string) on the uke or one key (black or white) on the piano.

* A whole step is the distance of two frets (along one string) on the uke or two keys (black or white) on the piano.

C Major Scale in Open Position

Although playing the C major scale entirely on string 3 is very instructive with regard to music intervals, it's very impractical, so let's learn a fingering for the scale in open position. If you need to brush up on how to read a scale box frame, refer to page 24. Since C is the tonic note of our scale, it's represented in the scale box frame as a hollow circle (or, in the case of an open string, a circle within a circle). The "L.H." numbers indicate which fingers you should use to fret the notes: index = 1, middle = 2, ring = 3, and pinky = 4.

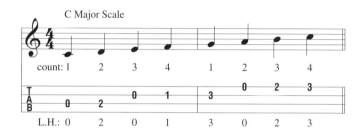

Slowly play through the notes of this scale from low to high, plucking with either your thumb or your index finger for now. All you should be concerned with right now is getting a clear sound from each note. Notice that your first finger should be used for all the first-fret notes, your second finger for the second-fret notes, and your ring finger for the third-fret notes. Pay special attention to this and be sure you're following the fingerings given. It's important to develop this habit early on, as it will pay dividends down the line.

- Place your fingers just behind the fret wire for each note.
- Keep your fingers arched and use the tip to make contact with the string.
- Keep all of your fingers hovering close to the fretboard, pressing one down when necessary. There's no need to lift your fingers far from the strings, as this will only slow you down.
- Keep your thumb on the back of the neck, providing gentle leverage against the fingers.

When you're ready, try playing it in the opposite direction, from top to bottom.

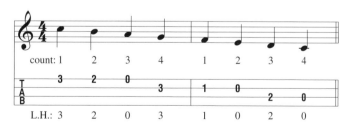

Make sure you're not allowing the first knuckle (the one nearest the fingertip) to bend backwards when playing these scales. You'll want to keep your fingers arched so that, should you need to play the adjacent string, you won't be deadening it accidentally with a flattened-out finger. Take extra care early in your development to avoid this bad habit.

OPEN-POSITION FRETBOARD MAP

Although it's not important at this point to know all the notes on the neck, we're going to give you a map of the fretboard in open position just as a reference. If, while playing any of the melodies or chords in this book, you'd like to know which note is which, you can refer back to this map and find out. Although the fourth string is rarely used in melodic playing (and isn't used at all in this chapter), it is, of course, used all the time in chordal playing, so it's included as well.

Notice that each "in between" note has two names: a flat version and a sharp version. The version that's used depends on music context (i.e., the key of the song and/or the direction of the melodic line, etc.).

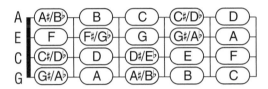

MELODIES IN C MAJOR

With the C major scale under your fingers, you're ready to play your first melodies. This is where the fun really begins! First up is "Twinkle, Twinkle Little Star," which contains a mixture of quarter notes and half notes.

Twinkle, Twinkle Little Star

If you're having trouble counting the rhythms even after reviewing the information on page 41, you can always listen to the audio tracks to hear how they're supposed to sound.

Next, let's try "Hot Cross Buns." Although we're only using three different notes here, we do have some eighth notes. The *tempo* (speed of the music) is still slow enough that it shouldn't pose too much of a problem, though.

Hot Cross Buns

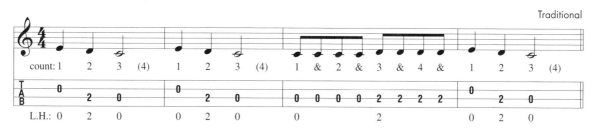

Now let's try a melody that uses all seven notes in the scale. We're back to quarter notes and half notes here.

Now let's try "Row, Row, Row Your Boat." This one's a bit trickier because it's in 6/8 meter instead of 4/4. This means there are six beats in each measure, and the eighth note is counted as the beat. It's usually counted so that beats 1 and 4 receive a bit more stress than the others. Try saying, "1–2–3–4–5–6" several times, and you should get the feel for it. One other new element is the *dotted quarter note*. When a *dot* appears after a note, it extends its value by half. So, a dotted quarter note takes up the same amount of time as a quarter note plus an eighth note, or three eighth notes. In 6/8, this aligns nicely with the stressed first and fourth eighth notes in each measure, which we'll see in this melody.

Row, Row, Row Your Boat

SONGS IN C MAJOR

Now let's put our C major scale to use with a few songs. First up is the classic cradle song "Brahms' Lullaby." This one is another new meter for us: 3/4. This is just like 4/4 but with one less beat per measure. Just count, "1–2–3, 1–2–3," etc., placing an emphasis on the first beat of each measure. This song uses every note of the C major scale and contains half notes, quarter notes, and eighth notes.

Do you notice anything special about the first measure of "Brahms' Lullaby?" There are only two eighth notes in it! So, what gives? Well, this song begins with two *pickup notes*. These are notes that precede the actual downbeat of the song and are therefore not given a full measure themselves.

So, when beginning this song, if you wanted to give yourself a bit of a runway, you could count "1-2-3, 1-2" and then start playing on beat 3. If you're ready to go right off the bat, you could just count "1-2" and then start. Either way, you start playing on beat 3.

Brahms' Lullaby

By Johannes Brahms

Next up is the Christmas favorite "Jingle Bells." This one is back in 4/4, but it makes use of a few eighth notes at a quicker tempo. There are also some dotted quarter notes here, so watch out for those and pay attention to the count. Take it as slowly as you need at first, making sure to give each note its full value.

Jingle Bells

Words and Music by J. Pierpont

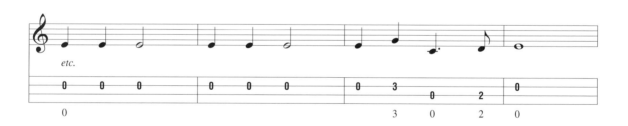

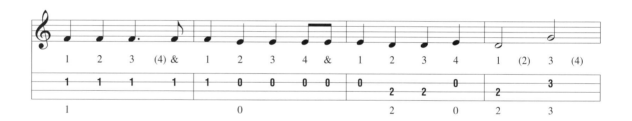

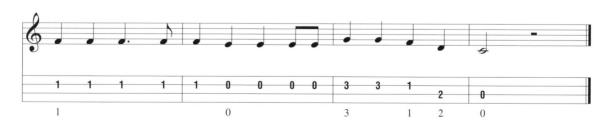

Now let's try the Frank Sinatra classic "Fly Me to the Moon," which also uses every note of the C major scale form. Before we do, though, let's learn another new musical symbol: the *tie*. A tie is a curved line (‿) that connects two notes, combining their durations into one. In other words, if you see a quarter note tied to another quarter note, the result will sound like a half note. If a quarter note is tied to an eighth note, the result with sound like a dotted quarter note, and so on.

One other thing about this song: It, like many jazzier songs, has a *swung eighths* feel. This means that the eighth notes sound lopsided, with the first in each beat sounding longer than the second. It's much easier to just listen to the audio to hear how it sounds because you'll immediately recognize the feel. Think of songs like "Happy Trails," "Pride & Joy" (Stevie Ray Vaughan), or "Jingle Bell Rock," as all of these songs use swung eighths as well. This feel is indicated by the little (♫=♩♪) symbol at the beginning of the music.

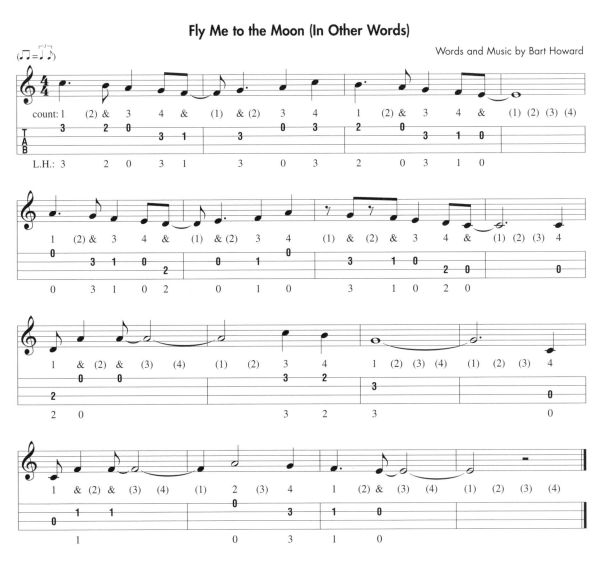

Fly Me to the Moon (In Other Words)

Words and Music by Bart Howard

And let's wrap it up with "Nowhere Man" by the Beatles. This one also uses all seven notes of the scale, with mostly quarter notes and half notes. There are a few dotted quarters and eighths, though, so watch out for them.

Nowhere Man

Words and Music by John Lennon and Paul McCartney

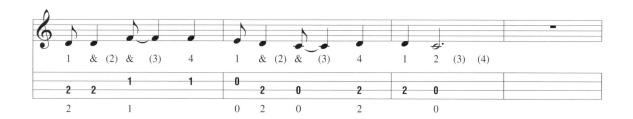

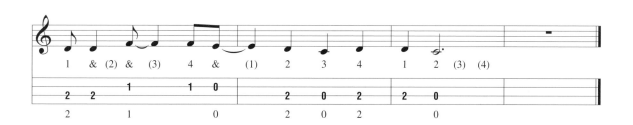

THE F MAJOR SCALE

Because the uke only has four strings *and* employs reentrant tuning, it has, compared to other instruments, quite a limited range—barely two full octaves, depending on your particular instrument and how far up the fretboard you consider playable (the 15th fret on string 1 would make for a two-octave range). This means that there aren't many scales that we can play in open position that encompass the full octave, low to high.

In fact, C major is the only major scale we can play from low to high without straying from open position. Of course, we can still play other major scales in open position; it's just that we can't play them from tonic to tonic the way we can with C major.

The F major scale is a case in point. We don't have a low F note—the lowest F note on the uke is on fret 1 of string 2—but we can play below it and above it to create a scale form that's still very useful for playing lots of melodies.

> Remember the key signature! The key signature for F major contains one flat, B♭. So, the notes in the F major scale are F–G–A–B♭–C–D–E. The B♭ is the only note that differs from the C major scale, which contains a B natural.

Here's how it looks:

 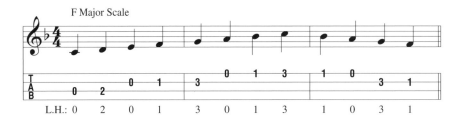

Notice that we came back down to the F note after reaching the high C note, so that we could end on the tonic.

> The *tonic* of a scale or key is "home base." It's the note that sounds resolved and the note after which the scale or key is named.

> The notes of a scale are often numbered from 1 to 7, in which 1 is the tonic. So, you could assign numbers to the C major scale as follows: C(1)–D(2)–E(3)–F(4)–G(5)–A(6)–B(7). By doing this, you can refer to notes by their numbers. For example, if we said "the 5th of C major," we would be referring to G. If we said "the 3rd of C," we'd be referring to E.
>
> The notes of the F major scale would be numbered the same way, only F would be 1, and there would be a B♭ instead of B: F(1)–G(2)–A(3)–B♭(4)–C(5)–D(6)–E(7). So, if we said "the 3rd of F," we'd be talking about A, and so on. Knowing this, we can say that this open-position F major scale form begins on the 5th (C), instead of the tonic (F), and extends to the 5th an octave higher.

So, why is a scale form like this useful? Well, as we'll soon see, certain melodies will fit better in a scale form like our C major form (tonic to tonic), but other melodies will fit better in a form like our F major form, which spans from 5th to 5th instead. (Be sure to read the previous **nuts & bolts** sidebar if you don't know what we mean by "5th to 5th.")

MELODIES IN F MAJOR

Now let's put our open-position F major scale form to work with a few melodies. First up is "Old MacDonald Had a Farm."

Old MacDonald Had a Farm

Traditional

Now let's try "Itsy Bitsy Spider," which is a bit more active and uses the swung-eighths feel. Listen to the audio track if you're still not clear on this.

Itsy Bitsy Spider

Traditional

Finally, here's "Hush, Little Baby," which contains a decent amount of eighth notes. The tempo is still pretty slow, though.

Hush, Little Baby

Carolina Folk Lullaby

When picking out melodies on your own, try using the C major form for ones in which the notes don't go below the tonic, such as "Brahms' Lullaby." For melodies with notes that dip below the tonic, such as "Old MacDonald," try the F major scale. Not all, but many melodies either span from tonic to tonic or from 5th to 5th, which is why these two scale forms are so useful.

SONGS IN F MAJOR

Now let's play a few tunes in our F major scale form. First up is Beethoven's "Ode to Joy." There are lots of quarter notes in this one, but there are a few eighth notes as well. Keep your foot tapping throughout!

The famous "Ode to Joy" chorus is derived from the fourth (and final) movement of Beethoven's ninth (and final) symphony, which he completed in 1824 (the lyrics come from the poem of the same name, written by German poet Friedrich Schiller in 1785). Despite being nearly deaf at the time of composition, the ninth symphony is largely heralded as one of Beethoven's greatest works.

Ode to Joy

Words by Henry van Dyke
Music by Ludwig van Beethoven

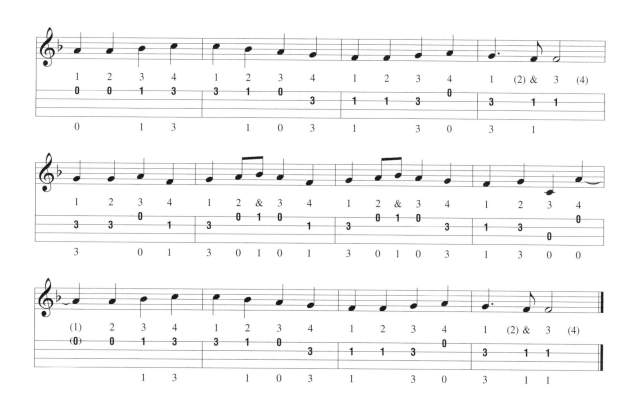

And now let's try "Happy Birthday to You." This one is in 3/4 and begins with two pickup notes. Also take note of measure 6, which contains a fermata. Earlier (on page 38) we said that a fermata indicates that you should hold a note for an indefinite amount of time. This often happens on the last note of a song—think of a final chord sustaining until it fades out. But fermatas can also occur in the middle of a song. Think about how people sing this song at a birthday party: They always draw out the person's name on that note for an extended period before finishing the song. This is exactly what a fermata sounds like in the middle of a song.

Happy Birthday to You

Words and Music by Mildred J. Hill and Patty S. Hill

Finally, let's play the Ritchie Valens classic "La Bamba." This one will have a few ties to watch out for, as well as some eighth notes. Also be sure to observe the rests!

La Bamba

By Richard Valenzuela

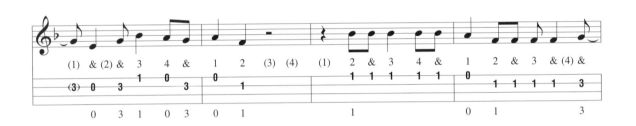

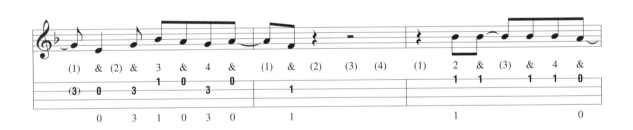

THE RELATIVE MINOR SCALE

Now that we know an F major scale, let's talk about the concept of the *relative minor*. First, let's play the notes of our F major scale from the tonic. We'll just play up five notes and then come back down.

It sounds happy and bright, right? But now let's try doing the same thing, only this time we'll start and end on a D note. In other words, we're still playing the notes of the F major scale, but we're going to start on D, play up five notes (to A), and come back to D.

All of a sudden it doesn't sound happy anymore, huh? It sounds sad and dark. Why is this? Well, it's because we're now tonicizing the note D, and therefore those notes sound as though they belong to the D minor scale. You see, the D minor scale and the F major scale contain exactly the same notes:

- **D minor scale**: D–E–F–G–A–B♭–C
- **F major scale**: F–G–A–B♭–C–D–E

These two scales just treat different notes as the tonic. This is the *relative* concept. We say that D minor is the relative minor of F major because they share the same notes and, therefore, the same key signature (one flat, B♭). Consequently, we can also say that F major is the relative major of D minor.

To help remember this *relative* concept, try thinking of two keys (one major and one minor) being "related" to each other because they share the same family of notes.

Every major scale has a relative minor scale, and vice versa. To find a major scale's relative minor, simply count to the 6th tone in the scale. We can confirm this with our F major scale: F(1)–G(2)–A(3)–B♭(4)–C(5)–**D(6)**–E(7). So, D minor is the relative minor of F major.

Let's try it with the other major scale we know, C major: C(1)–D(2)–E(3)–F(4)–G(5)–**A(6)**–B(7). So, A minor is the relative minor of C major.

The D Minor Scale

We can almost play the D minor scale from tonic to tonic in open position; we're just short by one note. So, we're going to reach up for that one note at the end to make it nice and tidy. However, since the uke's frets are so small, this won't be a problem.

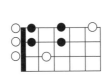

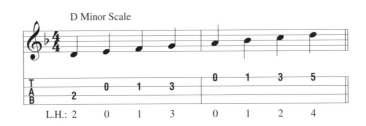

Notice the suggested fingering on the first string. For most people, it's easier to stretch between the index and the middle finger than it is to stretch between the ring finger and the pinky, but if you'd prefer to use a 1–3–4 fingering for that string, then go ahead.

Also note that, although we didn't play it in this form, the open third string (C) is within the D minor scale as well. (This makes sense, of course, considering the fact that C is in the F major scale, and the two scales share the same notes.) It is included in the scale box frame as a reminder that it can be accessed if necessary.

MELODIES AND SONGS IN D MINOR

Let's close out this chapter by playing a few tunes in our new D minor scale form. The first one is a brief, stately melody that makes use of the low C note (open third string).

The Christmas hymn "God Rest Ye Merry, Gentlemen" uses every note of the D minor scale, including the low C note below the tonic.

God Rest Ye Merry, Gentlemen

Traditional English Carol

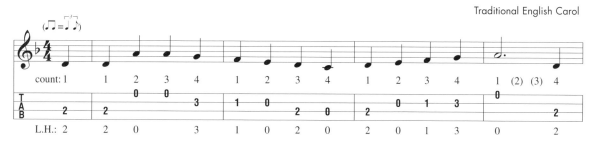

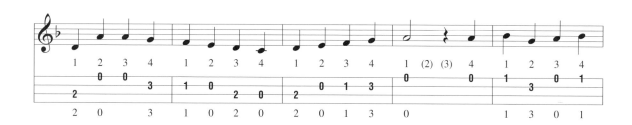

And let's close out with "St. James Infirmary Blues," which uses the swing-eighths feel.

St. James Infirmary Blues

Words and Music by Joe Primrose

"St. James Infirmary Blues," although popularized to great extent by Louis Armstrong's recording in 1928, is thought to have been derived from an English folk song from the 18th century called "The Unfortunate Rake." The title is thought to have referenced either the St. James Hospital (closed in 1532) or the St. James Workhouse (opened in 1725), both of which were in London.

More Advanced Playing

CHAPTER 8

SEVENTH CHORDS

What's Ahead:

- Open-position seventh chords
- Chord progressions with seventh chords
- More strumming patterns
- Chord-changing tricks
- Staccato strums

OK, so you've gotten a good bit under your fingers already. You can play lots of chords, two major scales, one minor scale, and lots of melodies. It's time to increase your chord vocabulary and open up a new world with *seventh chords*. We're also going to take a look at some more strumming concepts.

TRIAD REVIEW

If you remember, we said earlier that the chords we were playing were called *triads* because they contained three different notes (review the end of Chapter 5 if you missed it the first time). We can quickly expand on this since you learned about numbering scale tones in the last chapter. A triad contains a root (also called "1"), a 3rd, and a 5th. So, a C triad would contain a C, some kind of E (the 3rd), and some kind of G (the 5th).

C(1)–D(2)–E(3)–F(4)–G(5) = **C triad**: C–E–G

Notice that I said "some kind" of E (3rd) and G (5th). This is because there are different types of triads, and we alter the 3rd and/or 5th—that is, we lower (flat) or raise (sharp) them by a half step—to get these different types.

It so happens that, in the case of C, the triad we spelled above (C–E–G) was a C major triad. The other type of triad we learned was the minor triad, and we could turn that C major triad into a C minor triad by simply lowering the 3rd a half step.

- **C major triad:** C–E–G
- **C minor triad:** C–E♭–G

Notice that the root (C) and the 5th (G) are the same. The only difference between a major and minor triad is the 3rd. In a minor triad, the 3rd is always a half step lower than that of a major triad.

Don't worry too much about all this right now; it's not critical to know yet. The main point is to understand that chords are built by stacking notes this way (root–3rd–5th), as this is directly related to the topic at hand: seventh chords.

MAJOR SEVENTH CHORDS

Just as with triads, there are different types of seventh chords. But what's the difference between a seventh chord and a triad? It's simple. Whereas a triad has three different notes, a seventh chord has *four* different notes.

> The technical term for a seventh chord is *tetrad*. In other words, triad is to a three-note chord what tetrad is to a seventh chord. The term never caught on in the popular music world, however, and its use is limited mostly to schools and pedantic types.

A seventh chord contains a root, 3rd, 5th, and 7th. In the case of a *major seventh chord*, these notes are all drawn from the root's major scale. In other words, a Cmaj7 chord contains C, E, G, and B: the 1st, 3rd, 5th, and 7th notes of the C major scale.

Let's take a look at some different open-position seventh chords available to us on the uke.

> In a major seventh chord symbol, we add the suffix "maj7" after the uppercase letter. So, "Cmaj7" stands for "C major seven," "Gmaj7" stands for "G major seven," and so on.

Cmaj7, Gmaj7, B♭maj7, and Emaj7 Chords

Following are fingerings for four different major seventh chords in open position. For the first three (Cmaj7, Gmaj7, and B♭maj7), seeing the resemblance to their respective major triads should be easy. We didn't learn an E major chord yet because it requires a barre (we'll get to that in the next chapter), but Emaj7 can be played in open position.

For each chord, the major triad form is shown next to it so you can clearly see the connection. The Emaj7 chord is the exception. Notice that, for Gmaj7, an optional fingering that requires you to barre (flatten) your index finger across three strings is shown at the bottom. This is actually the most common fingering for Gmaj7, but it's listed as optional here because we won't officially look at barre chords until the next chapter.

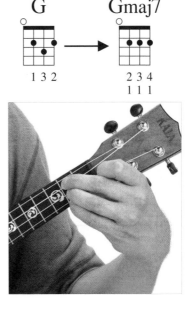

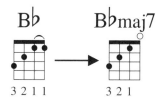

MAJOR SEVENTH CHORD PROGRESSIONS

Let's put these new chords to use in some progressions. This first one is in the key of G major and alternates G and Cmaj7 chords with a swung-eighths feel (also called a *shuffle feel*). Remember to watch for common tones. You don't need to move your middle finger from fret 2, string 1 at all here; it's in the same spot in both chords.

The strumming pattern is a slight variation of the last one we learned; now we're adding eighth notes on beat 4 as well. So, it's counted, "1, 2, 3-and, 4-and." Listen to the audio if you're having trouble with the shuffle feel.

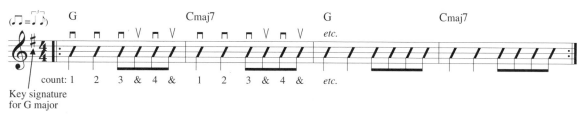

Here's another one in the key of G, this time making use of Gmaj7. Again, the eighth notes are swung for a bouncy feel.

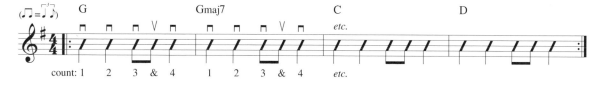

Syncopated Strum Patterns

Let's learn another new strum pattern, one that's got a twist in the form of *syncopation*. This term means that the weak beat is stressed. In a normal measure of 4/4, the first and third beats are normally stressed by default, and further on, the rest of the beats are generally stressed more than the "upbeats"—the "and" eighth notes in between the beats.

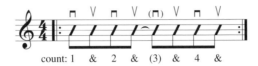

In this syncopated pattern, we're going to stress one of those upbeats by tying it to the next beat. So, the count looks like this: "1-and, 2-and, (3) and, 4-and," etc. In this case, the parenthetical "3" indicates a "missed" strum. And this brings us to the important part: You'll want to maintain the consistent down-up motion of your strumming finger throughout. The only difference between this pattern and strumming eighth notes for the entire measure is that you will purposefully miss the strings on beat 3. This is crucial, so be sure to get this right! You're laying the groundwork here for more complicated strumming patterns in the future in which you'll need your right hand to be the steady timekeeper—and you don't want to have to consciously think about it.

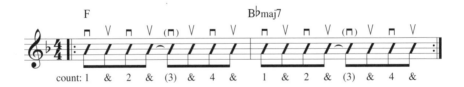

Here's another take on syncopation. In this type of pattern, the tempo would be faster than the previous pattern. We're stressing beat 2 in each measure by playing a half note there instead of a quarter note. Since we aren't using any eighth notes, you'll strum with all downstrokes.

This progression in E major (key signature of four sharps) alternates between Emaj7 and A chords. This is perhaps the most difficult chord change yet, so take it slowly at first. The Emaj7 chord isn't exactly easy to grab, so you'll really want to see it in your mind's eye before you reach for it.

Just so you know, if you ever see a major seventh chord in a song, you can always substitute a plain major triad instead. It might not have exactly the right sound, but it won't sound "wrong." You can think of a major seventh chord as a dressed-up major chord because it contains a major triad within it.

DOMINANT SEVENTH CHORDS

Next up are *dominant seventh chords*. Similar to major seventh chords, dominant seventh chords contain a major triad at their base. However, whereas major seventh chords add a major 7th note on top, dominant seventh chords add a minor 7th, or ♭7th, note on top. This makes them sound completely different; most people consider them funky, bluesy, or tense.

You hear dominant seventh chords in all kinds of popular music, most frequently in blues, classic rock, funk, and jazz. Think of the opening chord in "Born on the Bayou"—that's a dominant seventh chord. You'll also hear them in lots of songs by James Brown, the Beatles, the Rolling Stones, and virtually every blues artist out there.

C7, G7, A7, E7, and D7 Chords

The suffix for a dominant seventh chord is simply "7," So, "C7" stands for "C dominant seven," and so on. Again, for each chord below, the corresponding major triad is shown, with the exception of E.

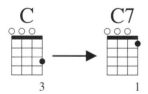

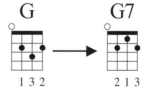

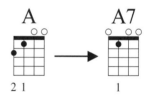

E7

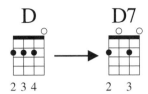

1 2 3

2 3 4   2 3

It's always a good idea to compare these chords with similar, previous ones. In this case, notice how the dominant seventh chords differ from the major seventh chords. You'll find that, in each case, one note has been lowered by a half step. This note is the 7th of the chord. If you remember, we said that major seventh chords contained a root, 3rd, 5th, and major 7th. Dominant sevenths, however, contain a root, 3rd, 5th, and ♭7th. And that's confirmed when we compare the major seventh and dominant seventh voicings.

DOMINANT SEVENTH CHORD PROGRESSIONS

Now let's put our new chords to use in a few more progressions.

In this next example, notice the dots appearing above the slashes. These are *staccato* markings and they indicate that the notes (or in this case, chords) should be played in a short, clipped manner. This means that you need to stop them from ringing right after strumming them. If you aren't using any open strings, you only need to release the pressure with your left hand. However, since these chords contain open strings, you'll need to stop the strings by touching them in between the strums with your plucking hand. This may feel a little awkward at first, but soon you won't even have to think about it.

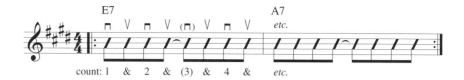

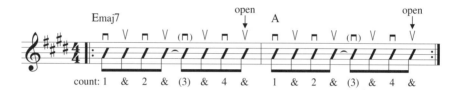

The Chord Change "Cheat"

You may have noticed in a few examples, such as the previous one, that it's very difficult to change chords smoothly in the space of an eighth note. Since you've stuck with us this far, we'll let you in on a little secret: Oftentimes, we're *not* actually doing that! What I mean is that we're "cheating" a bit.

Take the previous example. Instead of holding down the E7 chord for the entire measure and then quickly jumping to A7, you can actually start to re-fret for the new chord on the last eighth note of the measure and just strum a few open strings on the upstroke to maintain the illusion of continuity.

Keep in mind that this isn't always necessary. If the tempo is slow enough, it may be easy to make the chord change in time. Or if the chords share common tones, that usually helps as well. But if two chords require you to completely lift up and re-fret, and the tempo is clipping along, then the open-string cheat can be the answer.

Whereas moving from E7 to A7 might be doable, the move from Emaj7 to A on page 63 is much more difficult and a prime candidate for this "cheat" when strumming with eighth notes.

MINOR SEVENTH CHORDS

The third type of seventh chord we'll look at is the *minor seventh*. Just as the major seventh and dominant seventh chords were based off the major triad (i.e., they contained a major triad within them), the minor seventh chord, as you may have suspected, is based off the minor triad. It contains a root, ♭3rd, 5th, and ♭7th.

Minor seventh chords sound a bit more sophisticated or mysterious than minor triads. They're a bit more of a chameleon, though, because they can sound funky, gritty, or pretty, depending on the context. You can hear them in a lot of popular classic rock songs, such as "Long Train Runnin'" by the Doobie Brothers, in which they sound a bit gritty, or "You Never Give Me Your Money" by the Beatles and "Crash" by Dave Matthews Band, in which they sound pretty.

Am7, Dm7, Gm7, and Em7 Chords

The chord suffix for a minor seventh chord is "m7." So, "Am7" refers to "A minor seven." As you play through the following chords, remember to compare the first three to the minor triad versions you learned in Chapter 6. Although we didn't learn an Em chord then, we'll add one now. It puts your hand in second position (i.e., your index finger is on fret 2), but it still contains an open string and is easy to play.

Am7 is *the* easiest chord on the uke to play, hands down (and we mean that literally!). Notice that Dm7, while still played in the same area as Dm, doesn't contain an open string. This means that it's technically in first position because your index finger is at the first fret. And for the Gm7 chord, you'll barre your index finger across strings 1 and 2, just as with the B♭ chord.

extras

The term "position" refers to the location of your index finger on the uke neck. If you're playing a chord in which your index finger is on fret 3, then you're in third position, and so on.

The term we've been using thus far, "open position," generally means that at least one open string is included and all your fingers are within the first few frets. However, you will occasionally hear a chord like F major described as "first position" because your index finger is on fret 1, even though it also contains open strings. Or you could hear G major described as "second position," even though it contains an open string. When no open strings are included, however, you always label the position using the index finger.

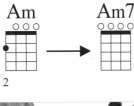

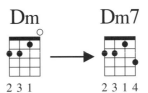

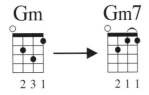

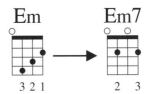

Although some chord fingerings are set in stone, many of them are merely suggestions based on what's conventionally used. But remember that you can alter them if it helps make a particular chord change smoother.

Take the Em7 chord above, for example. It shows 2 and 3 for the fingering, and this is perfectly comfortable on its own. But if you were alternating between a G chord and Em7, it would make more sense to use fingers 1 and 2 for the Em7 because those would be common to the G chord.

MINOR SEVENTH CHORD PROGRESSIONS

Triplet Strum Patterns

Let's expand our rhythmic palette now by looking at triplets. A *triplet* is a rhythm in which three notes are placed in the space normally occupied by two. For example, instead of normal eighth notes, like this:

Triplets will divide the beat into three equal parts, like this:

Notice that there are two common methods for counting triplets. Some prefer to say, "1 & a, 2 & a, etc.," while others say, "1-trip-let, 2-trip-let, etc." They both work equally well, so it's just a matter of personal preference.

With regard to strumming triplets, there are, again, various methods used. For slow-to-moderate tempos, a down-up-down method works well. Try that out with this progression in D minor that moves between Dm7 and Am7. Try to *accent* the first strum in each beat (i.e., strum a little bit harder).

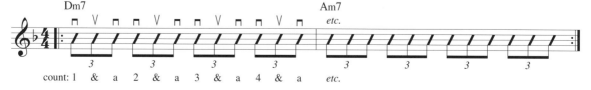

This progression in G major mixes quarter notes with triplet strums. Pay attention to the strum indicators. Beats 3 and 4 in each measure use the same strum pattern as the previous example.

Now let's add some eighth notes, using a shuffle (swung-eighths) feel. This may sound complicated, but it's actually pretty natural-sounding. You see, you may not have realized it, but you were actually playing with a triplet feel earlier when you used the shuffle feel. Two eighth notes played with a shuffle feel are actually equivalent to the first and third notes of a triplet.

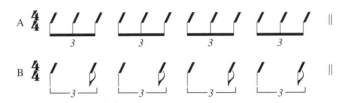

In fact, line B above sounds exactly like shuffled (or "swung") eighth notes. It's just a different way of notating it. So, let's try alternating between a measure of swung eighth notes and a measure of triplets with a progression in F major. Notice the swung-eighths indication at the beginning. Also notice that there are two strum choices for measure 1. The top row would be more appropriate for quicker tempos, whereas the bottom row may feel better for slower tempos. If you think about it, the bottom row is the same as the triplet strum, only that you're "missing" the middle strum in each beat.

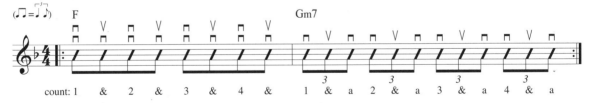

Finally, let's tie it all together here with a mixture of quarter notes, eighth notes, and triplets, using a shuffle feel in a C major progression. Watch the strum indicators and the counts.

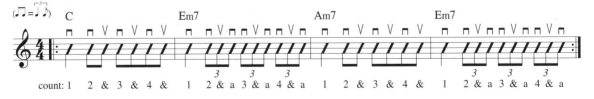

Of course, at faster tempos, it gets harder to perform two downstrokes in a row. In that case, you can resort to alternating down-up strums throughout the triplets. The hardest thing about this is maintaining the accents on the downbeats throughout. Downstrokes tend to sound more accented than upstrokes by default, so you will need to consciously strum a bit harder on the upstrokes that fall on beats 2 and 4. This is indicated in the music with an accent symbol (>) as a reminder.

Also realize that the following example is the perfect spot to employ the open-string "cheat" we talked about on page 65. If you listen closely to the audio, you can hear the open strings being strummed on the very last triplet of each measure. If we didn't do this, it would be nearly impossible to make the chord changes cleanly and in time.

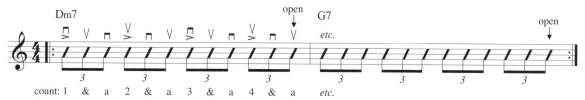

Substitution Possibilities

We said earlier that seventh chords are kind of like dressed-up triads. They have a more specific sound that can often be just what a song needs. Here are some guidelines with regard to their interchangeability for you to use as a reference:

- A major triad can always be substituted for a major seventh or dominant seventh chord. It will most likely sound a bit blander, but you won't hit any wrong notes.

- A major seventh chord can be substituted for a major chord if it's on the 1st or 4th degree of the tonic scale. In other words, the key of C major looks like this: C(1)–D(2)–E(3)–F(4)–G(5)–A(6)–B(7). There are three diatonic (i.e., "in key") major triads in every key (just trust us on this for now); these are the first, fourth, and fifth chords of the key. In C, this means C, F, and G. So, Cmaj7 can substitute for C, and Fmaj7 can substitute for F, but Gmaj7 usually can't substitute for G. (It's not that you'll never see it happen, but it's not a diatonic chord, and therefore will draw attention to itself.)

- A dominant seventh chord can always substitute for a major chord when it's built from the fifth chord of the key. In our C major example, G is the fifth chord in the key, so G7 can always substitute for G in that case.

- A dominant seventh chord can sometimes substitute for the first and fourth chords in a key if it's a bluesy of funky song. So in C major, C7 can possibly substitute for C, and F7 can possibly substitute for F. You'll just have to use your ear to decide if it works.

- Minor seventh chords and minor triads are always interchangeable; just use your ears to decide what sounds better.

- You know three types of seventh chords: major seventh (maj7), dominant seventh (7), and minor seventh (m7).

- A triplet divides a beat into three equal parts.

- Shuffled eighth notes are triplets that are "missing" the middle strum in each beat.

- The "open-string cheat" is a great way to smooth over a difficult chord change.

CHAPTER 9

BARRE CHORDS AND MOVEABLE CHORD FORMS

What's Ahead:
- A-based barre chords
- C-based barre chords
- F-based barre chords
- E-based barre chords
- Other moveable forms
- Barre-chord progressions

Although we've tinkered with barres a bit—with our B♭ and Gm7 chords, for instance—it's time to push off the ice rink wall for good and try skating on our own. That's right; we're leaving open position! (Just temporarily, of course—we'll always have a home there.) The good news is that barre chords on the uke are pretty easy. In fact, compared to a guitar, they're a breeze!

THE WONDERFUL WORLD OF BARRE CHORDS
The benefits of barre chord forms can't be overstated. Simply put, they allow you to play *any* chord in *any* key in numerous places on the neck. If you don't like one particular voicing, don't worry—there's another one a few frets away that may suit your fancy. Most barre chords involve flattening your index finger across three or four strings while using your other fingers in front of it to create chord forms.

What's important to realize is that barre chords didn't just fall from the sky; every barre chord form is based off an open chord shape. This becomes apparent when you treat the open strings as "zero frets." Let's see how this works…

A-BASED BARRE CHORDS
If you look at an open A chord, you'd probably think, "Two open strings and notes on strings 4 and 3." This is true of course, but what happens if you imagine those open strings as "zero frets" that need to be played with fingers?

A-Form Major Barre Chords
To play the A chord with the method describe above, you'd need a finger to lay across strings 1 and 2 behind the nut, and then you'd have to use your ring and middle fingers for strings 4 and 3, respectively, which would look like this:

A

3 2 1 1

Now take that same exact shape and move everything up one fret. What do you get? A B♭ chord!

So, B♭ is actually an A-based barre chord! But let's not stop there. If you move it up one more fret, you'll get a B chord. One more fret from there gives you a C chord, and on and on.

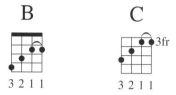

Notice that, for the C chord, we've abandoned the open position in our chord grid and started using fret markers to identify the position of the chord. In this case, "3fr" indicates third position.

The good news is that we can slide this form up or down the neck to play almost any chord—we say "almost" because the farther up the neck you go, the less comfortable it is. But don't worry about that. Together with the other barre-chord forms we'll learn, we can easily cover any chord.

Fretboard Map: Strings 4 and 1

In order to play different chords, you'll need to know where to place your fingers. This means you'll need to learn the notes on the neck. At this point, it will be helpful to at least learn the note names along the fourth string because that's where the chord roots are located in the A-based barre form. So, study this diagram and commit it to memory as soon as you can:

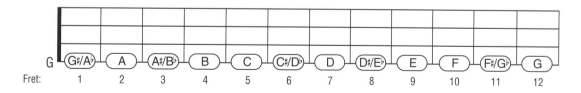

Notice that we start at the open string with G. By the time we reach fret 12, we're back to G again, only one octave higher this time. In between, we're just moving straight up the *chromatic scale*, which includes all 12 notes. In other words, if you start at G on a piano and start moving to the right, playing every key along the way (black and white) until you reach the next G, these are the notes you'd get. Also notice that our natural half steps are still there. In other words, there's no note between B and C and between E and F; they're each one fret apart.

So, by knowing the notes along this string, we can now slide that A-based form up and down the neck to play just about any chord. Just make sure your ring finger is on the root note you want, and you've got it!

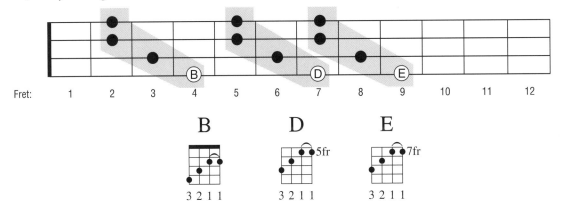

And there's more good news. In case you hadn't noticed yet when playing through your chords, the notes on string 4 and string 1 of this chord form are *exactly* the same (because of the reentrant tuning, they even sound in the same octave). This means that you can use this form to learn the notes on string 1, as well:

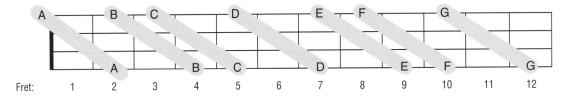

A-Form Minor Barre Chords

We can also use the Am chord to generate a minor version of this barre form. Just re-finger the open Am chord, using your ring finger on string 4 and barring your index behind the nut.

Move it up one fret, and you have a B♭m chord.

The only difference between a major chord and minor chord is that the 3rd of the chord has been lowered a half step. In the case of an A chord, A major contains A (root), C♯ (3rd), and E (5th). An Am chord therefore contains A (root), C (♭3rd), and E (5th).

A-FORM BARRE CHORD PROGRESSIONS

Now that you've got the major and minor A-form barre chords under your belt, let's play through some progressions using both. The chord's fret position will be indicated below the staff to remind you that we're using barre forms. This first one is in C major and alternates between C and Dm chords.

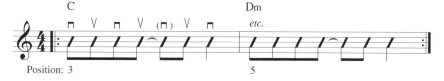

This one uses a shuffle feel, and some of the chords are played staccato. However, since you're using barre chords with no open strings, all you have to do to create the staccato effect is quickly release the fret pressure after you strum—you don't even have to worry about deadening the strings with your right hand.

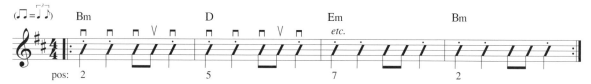

A-Form Seventh Barre Chords

We can turn our open A7 and Am7 chords into barre-chord forms the same way:

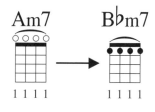

Let's put these seventh-chord barre forms to use with some progressions. Watch out for the staccato markings and ties!

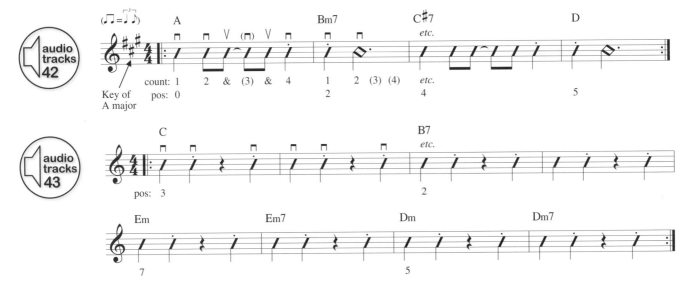

C-BASED BARRE CHORDS

We can create barre chords from other open chords as well, such as the open C chord. Let's look at that now. The process is the same as before.

C-Form Major Barre Chords

First, re-finger the open chord by thinking of the open strings as zero frets that need to be played. This would make your open C chord look like the grid shown here:

Slide that up one fret, and you have a Db (or C#) barre chord.

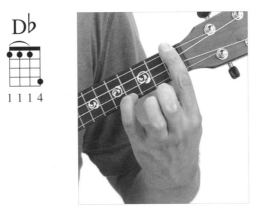

Although it is possible to play a minor form of this barre chord, it's not terribly comfortable, so we'll skip it for now.

C-Form Seventh Barre Chords

Major seventh and dominant sevenths are a breeze with this form; you just move the note on string 1 down: One fret for the major seventh and two frets for the dominant seventh.

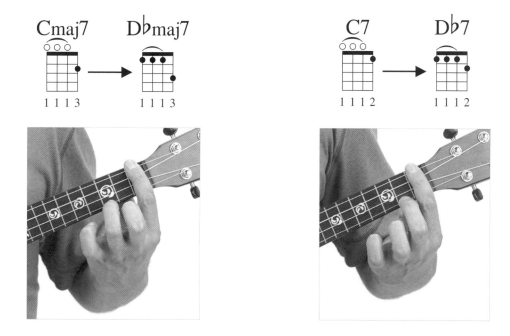

The minor seventh barre chord in this form is playable as well, and you actually learned it already; it's the Dm7 chord form you learned back on page 66. While this is technically not a barre chord (because no fingers are barred), it is a *moveable* form because it contains no open strings. So for instance, if we slide that Dm7 chord up two frets, we have Em7:

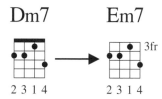

Fretboard Map: String 3

For the C-based major form, the root of the chord is found on strings 3 and 1 (the note on string 1 is an octave higher than the note on string 3, but it's the same note). For the C-based seventh forms, however, the root is only found on string 3. So let's create a fretboard map to learn the notes on string 3.

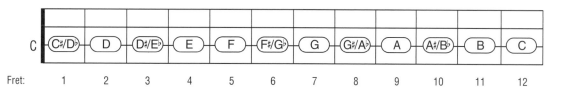

We learned the notes on string 1 earlier, but we can use this chord form to see how they relate to the notes on string 3.

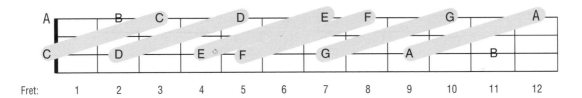

C-FORM BARRE CHORD PROGRESSIONS

We'll now put our C-form barre chords to use in some progressions. This will include the major, major seventh, dominant seventh, and minor seventh forms.

16th-Note Strum Patterns

For these progressions, let's learn another new rhythm: the *16th note*. Simply put, it's twice as fast as the eighth note. This is also represented visually, as the 16th has an extra flag (♪) or beam when played in succession (♫♫) as compared to the eighth note. There are 16 in a measure of 4/4 time, or four per beat. When you strum constant 16th notes, you use alternate down- and up-strums.

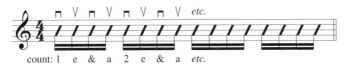

When you're playing a pattern that's based on eighth notes and 16th notes (as is often the case when 16ths are used), you'll use downstrokes for all the eighth notes and only upstrokes when playing 16ths. It's as if you've double-timed the strategy used for quarter and eighth notes.

Let's check it out in this D major progression. Watch the strum indications closely.

In this next example, we're using a common combination of eighths and 16ths called a "gallop," which consists of one eighth followed by two 16ths (♪♫). Watch out for beat 3 in measures 2 and 4 though, as the rhythm changes slightly. Also, we're adding syncopation here by changing chords on the last eighth note of measures 1 and 3 and allowing the chord to ring over the bar line. This is another common syncopation technique. Take note of the staccato marks!

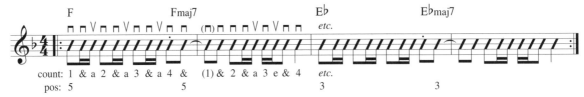

F-BASED AND E-BASED BARRE CHORDS

Finally, we can build barre chords from our open F chord as well.

F-Form Major Barre Chords

Let's use the same process to turn our F major chord into a barre:

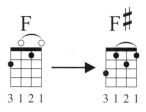

Fretboard Map: String 2

For the F chord form, the root is found on string 2. Since this is the only string we haven't mapped out yet, let's do that now.

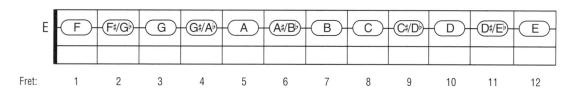

So, by placing the root where you want along string 2, you can move the F-form major barre chord around.

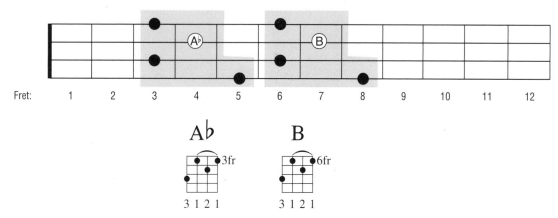

F-Form Minor Barre Chords

We didn't look at an open Fm chord, but that doesn't mean we can't easily turn our major barre shape into a minor one. All we need to do is lower the notes on strings 1 and 4, both of which are the chord's 3rd, down a half step. In the diagrams below, the roots of the chords are shown as open circles.

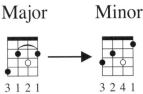

You can see now why we didn't have an open F minor chord like this; we couldn't go lower than the open strings. Note that this new form is not a barre chord but simply a moveable form. Once you consult the fretboard map for string 2, you can move this minor form around.

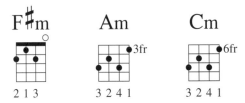

E-Form Seventh Barre Chords

We've grouped F-based and E-based barre chords here because they're really the same form, but because of the open strings, we couldn't play these F-form seventh chords in open position. We could play them as E-form seventh chords though, so that's why they're named as such. Note that only the minor seventh is a barre chord; the other two are simply moveable forms.

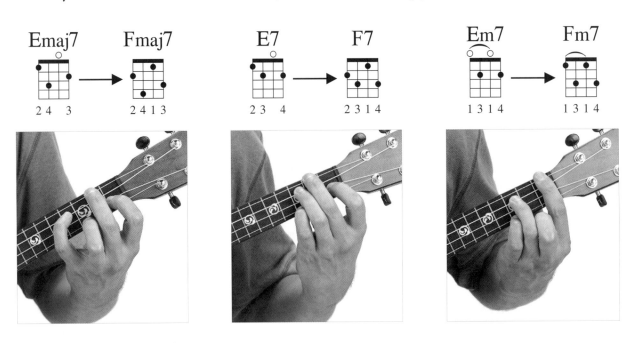

On more difficult chords, such as Fmaj7 and Fm7, pluck the chord one string at a time to make sure that all of the notes are ringing clearly. If any note sounds choked or buzzy, this method will always make it obvious.

F-FORM/E-FORM BARRE CHORD PROGRESSIONS

Let's check out our new chord forms in action. This first example is in the key of A♭ major, which has four flats (B♭, E♭, A♭, and D♭) in its key signature. We're using a shuffle feel here, with lots of staccato strums.

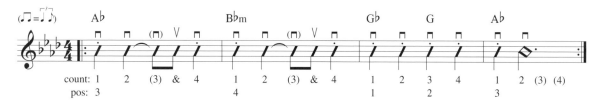

Here's a funky-sounding one in G. Watch the rhythms closely; there are a lot of rests that have to be acknowledged. As always, listen to the audio track to clear up any trouble spots.

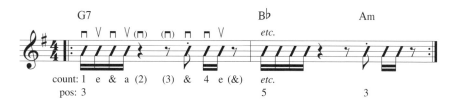

Remember: Any chord that doesn't use open strings is moveable (i.e., the form can be moved up or down the neck to play it from any root), and barre chords are not the only chords that are moveable.

OTHER MOVEABLE FORMS

We'll look at a few more useful moveable forms here that are based off the open D and open G chords.

D-Form Major and Minor Chords

These are technically not barre chords because we're not using a barre, but they're still very useful forms, particularly the minor one.

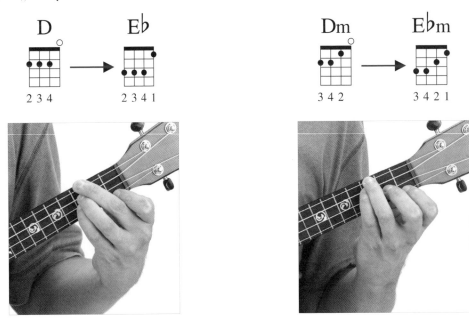

G-Form Seventh Chords

The open G form generates some great moveable seventh chords.

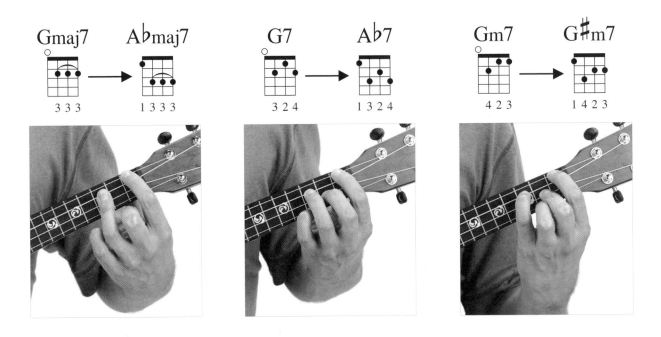

COMBINING ALL THE FORMS

Let's finish off the chapter with some progressions that make use of all the barre forms we've learned thus far. Anything goes! This is actually where the true benefit lies (i.e., being able to play just about any chord, at any place on the neck). We'll see in these progressions that, with all of these chord forms under your fingers, there's no need to move all over the neck unless you want to. Since we're mixing all the forms together here, the chord grids will be shown for each voicing.

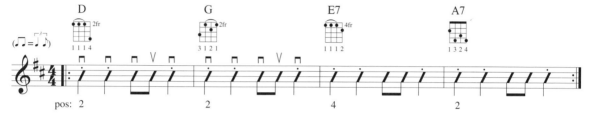

This example in G minor uses several different rhythms, so watch closely. We're also changing chords on the last eighth note in measure 1. And don't miss the staccato mark on beat 3 of measure 2!

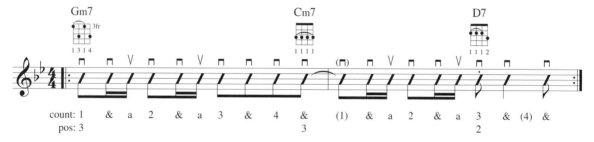

- All barre chord and moveable chord forms are based off open chord forms.
- When playing a 16th-note-based strum pattern, keep your strumming hand moving downward on every eighth note, adding any in-between 16th notes with upstrokes.
- You can add syncopation to your strum patterns by either changing chords on a weak beat and/or sustaining a weak beat chord strum over a strong beat. The "and" of beat 2 and the "and" of beat 4 are both common syncopations.

CHAPTER 10

CHAPTER 10
PENTATONIC SCALES

What's Ahead:

- Open-position C major and F major pentatonic scale patterns
- Open-position A minor and D minor pentatonic scale patterns
- Moveable major pentatonic scale patterns
- Moveable minor pentatonic scale patterns
- Major and minor pentatonic licks
- Hammer-ons, pull-offs, and slides

OK, so you've got lots of chords under your belt, as well as some scales and simple melodies. Now it's time to concentrate on playing some "lead" ukulele.

LIKE THE BACK OF YOUR HAND

When it comes to solos—especially in blues, rock, and country styles—the pentatonic scale is the most common scale of them all; you know the sound like the back of your hand. Just name a classic rock song and chances are it'll be packed with pentatonic riffs and/or solos. A tiny sampling could consist of "Back in Black" by AC/DC, "Stairway to Heaven" or "Black Dog" by Led Zeppelin, "Let It Be" by the Beatles, "Honky Tonk Women" by the Rolling Stones, "Jet Airliner" by the Steve Miller Band, and on and on. In the blues field, you'll hear it in "The Thrill Is Gone" by B.B. King, "Pride & Joy" by Stevie Ray Vaughan, "Born Under a Bad Sign" by Albert King, "Hideaway" by Freddie King, and countless others. And the pentatonic scale can also be heard in countless country songs like "Guitars, Cadillacs" by Dwight Yoakam, "Blue Moon of Kentucky" by Bill Monroe, "Mountain Music" by Alabama, and "The Claw" by Jerry Reed, to name but a few. In short, the pentatonic scale is simply a must-learn scale.

WHAT IS THE PENTATONIC SCALE?

There are two types of pentatonic scales: the *major pentatonic* and the *minor pentatonic*. They're created by eliminating two notes from their seven-note cousins—the major scale and the minor scale, respectively. The reason that these scales are so common is that they only contain relatively "safe" notes. In other words, all of the notes in the scale are pretty consonant (i.e., they sound good) and therefore require less care with regard to properly resolving notes.

A prime example of this is the 4th degree of a major scale. In C major, this would be the F note: C(1)–D(2)–E(3)–**F(4)**. This note, while very useful, can also sound quite bad when it's not handled properly. If you land on the F note while playing over a C chord, for example, it's usually not going to sound very good. The major pentatonic scale, however, omits this 4th note (as well as one more), so you don't have to worry about it.

Want an easy way to hear a pentatonic scale? Just find a piano and play only the black keys! You'll be playing the notes of the F♯ major pentatonic or D♯ minor (the relative minor) pentatonic scale.

THE MAJOR PENTATONIC SCALE

Let's look at the major pentatonic first. To create this scale, we eliminate the 4th and 7th notes of the major scale. If you remember, we've learned two major scales so far: C major and F major. So let's take a look at how we turn those into major pentatonic scales.

The Open-Position C Major Pentatonic Scale

Starting with C major, let's see how we turn it into C major pentatonic. Again, we remove the 4th and 7th notes. In the C major scale, those are the notes F and B.

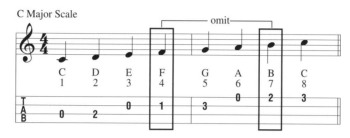

After removing those two notes, we're left with the C major pentatonic scale in open position.

Try playing the major scale and the major pentatonic scale back to back to hear the difference. Notice how the notes of the major pentatonic scale don't have the amount of tension created by the 4th (F) and 7th (B). In other words, when you play the F or B note, they don't really sound stable; they want to resolve to a nearby consonant note.

The Open-Position F Major Pentatonic Scale

We create the F major pentatonic scale the same way (i.e., by omitting the 4th and 7th degrees of the F major scale). If you remember, our open-position F major scale spanned from the 5th (C) to the 5th, and the only note that differed from C major was B♭ (which is indicated in the key signature). So, we need to remove the 4th and 7th notes of the F major scale, which is not the same as the 4th and 7th notes of this scale form, since we're not starting on the tonic. The F major scale is F(1)–G(2)–A(3)–B♭(4)–C(5)–D(6)–E(7), so we need to remove B♭ (4th) and E (7th).

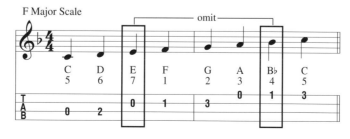

After we've done that, we're left with F major pentatonic in open position. Again, as when we first learned the F major scale, we'll come back down to the tonic again at the end.

F Major Pentatonic Scale

The exact origin of the pentatonic scale is unknown, but we do know that it is incredibly ancient. In fact, many bone flutes have been found around the world, with holes tuned to the pentatonic scale, that are believed to be 40,000–60,000 years old.

Some theories suggest that this five-tone scale is related to the "number of man," a concept dating to ancient times thought to do with the fact that we have five fingers, or perhaps the fact that we have four limbs and one head. Others suggest that it has to do with the five observable planets (to the naked eye): Mercury, Venus, Mars, Jupiter, and Saturn.

Whatever the reason, it's clear that these five tones have a powerful significance, as the pentatonic scale is ubiquitous in countless cultures, past and present.

OPEN-POSITION MAJOR PENTATONIC LICKS

A *lick* is (usually) a short musical phrase used to create solos. Oftentimes, a solo is the result of stringing together many licks to make a longer musical statement. Just as we combine different words from our vocabulary to form sentences and paragraphs on the spot, a musical improviser uses licks from his/her musical vocabulary to form complete solos. Let's learn a few major pentatonic licks now. As with the melodies we learned in Chapter 7, you can pluck the notes with your thumb or index finger.

C Major Pentatonic Licks

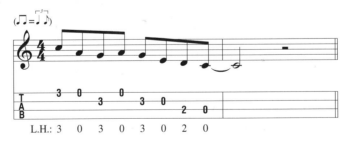

The rhythm is a little tricky on this next one, so listen to the audio track to make sure you've got the syncopation right.

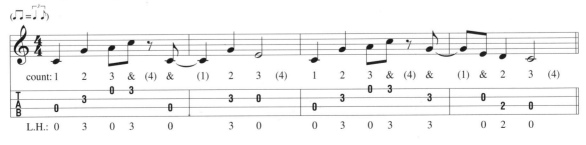

There are a few things to watch out for on the next lick. First is the dotted-eighth-note rhythm. You're playing the first 16th notes of the beat but sustaining the second one for the rest of the beat. The second thing is the staccato markings on beat 3 of each measure. Since it's an open string, you'll need to pluck it and then immediately touch it with the plucking finger to stop it from ringing. Fortunately, you're plucking that same note again, so it's not too difficult. This is a subtle effect, but these subtleties are what can turn these notes from just scales into actual music.

Hammer-Ons and Pull-Offs

Hammer-ons and pull-offs are used to create a smooth, connected sound in our phrases. The musical term for this is *legato*. Think of a violin. They can either play two notes on one string by bowing down for one note and up for the other, or they can simply play both notes by using the same down bow. In the former, we'd hear the attack of the bow again for the second note; in the latter, we would only hear the notes change with no second bow attack. This is kind of analogous to hammer-ons and pull-offs on the ukulele.

To perform a *hammer-on*, you pluck one note and then "hammer" down to a higher fret on the same string to sound the next note (without plucking). The first (plucked) note can be an open string or a fretted note, but the second note will always be a fretted one.

Let's try the technique by hammering from the open third string (C) to the D note at fret 2. You'll need to use a swift hammering motion and then maintain pressure once you come down on the fret. In the music, a *slur* is used to show a hammer-on. A slur looks just like a tie, but it connects two notes of the same pitch, while a slur connects two different notes.

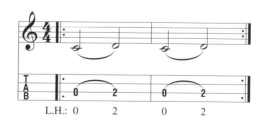

Now try hammering from F at fret 1, string 2 to G at fret 3, string 2. Again, the secret is using a swift, controlled hammering motion.

Just because the hammering motion needs to be swift doesn't mean that you should lift the hammering finger far away from the fretboard. That will only lead to less accuracy, and it will slow you down. Your hammering finger doesn't need to be more than a half inch off the fretboard before performing the hammer motion.

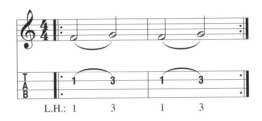

A *pull-off* is sort of the opposite of a hammer-on; you want to pluck the first note and then sound a lower note on the same string by "pulling off" the fretting finger toward the floor. Essentially, you're using that fretting finger to pluck the string.

In this first example, we'll pull off from the D note at fret 2 on string 3 to the open third string (C). After plucking the D note, pull the finger off the string in a downward fashion so that it comes to rest against string 2. The release needs to be swift and clean in order to produce a strong pull-off. Again, there's no need for the pull-off finger to fly way off the fretboard.

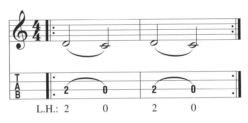

Don't press too hard when executing a pull-off, as this can cause the note to go sharp just before you release the string. Use normal fretting pressure and then quickly move down and off the string.

And now let's try pulling off from G at fret 3 of string 2 to F at fret 1. For this move, you'll need to have your first finger on the F note before pulling off from the G note with your ring finger. Because of this, pull-offs—when using two fretted notes—require a bit more preparation than hammer-ons.

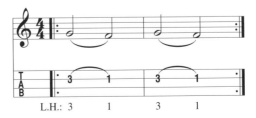

F Major Pentatonic Licks

Let's make use of hammer-ons and pull-offs in some F major pentatonic licks.

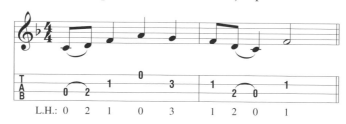

Watch the rhythm on this next one. We're adding syncopation at the end of measure 1 by sustaining that high C note over the bar line before pulling it off. Listen to the audio track if this is confusing.

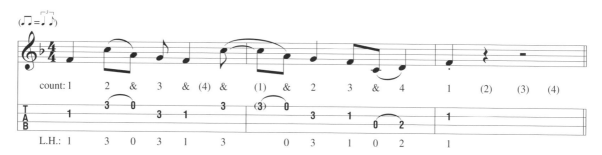

This next lick features two pickup 16th notes in a common move. The tempo is pretty slow here, so it's not as difficult as it first looks.

This last example shows why hammer-ons and pull-offs are so useful: They really allow you to add some speed to your melody playing. The audio track for this example features two different tempos: One at a slow speed and one at a faster speed to demonstrate the effectiveness of hammer-ons and pull-offs in this manner.

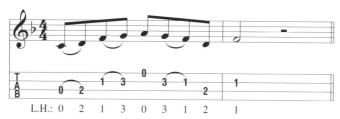

THE MINOR PENTATONIC SCALE

Just as the major pentatonic scale omits two notes from the major scale, the minor pentatonic scale omits two notes from the minor scale: The 2nd and 6th.

The Open-Position A Minor Pentatonic Scale

Although we didn't look at the A minor scale in Chapter 7, we can do so now with the new knowledge we've gained about relative minors. Remember that we said relative minor and major scales share the same notes; the only difference is which note is treated as the tonic.

The relative minor of C major is A minor, and we can confirm this by counting up six notes of the C major scale: C(1)–D(2)–E(3)–F(4)–G(5)–**A(6)**–B(7). Therefore, C major pentatonic and A minor pentatonic share the same notes. If you'd like a more robust explanation of that rather than taking it at face value, we can do that…

The A minor scale is spelled A(1)–B(2)–C(3)–D(4)–E(5)–F(6)–G(7). Above, we said that you create a minor pentatonic scale by eliminating the 2nd and 6th notes of a minor scale. What are the 2nd and 6th notes of the A minor scale? That would be B(2) and F(6). And which two notes did we eliminate from the C major scale to create the C major pentatonic? That's right! B and F. So we can conclusively say that C major pentatonic and A minor pentatonic share the same five notes: C, D, E, G, and A. If you treat C as the tonic, it's a C major pentatonic scale; if you treat A as the tonic, it's an A minor pentatonic scale.

Therefore, we can use the same open-position C major pentatonic scale to play in A minor pentatonic as well. We just treat A as the tonic, which means we'll resolve most of our phrases to A instead of C.

A Minor Pentatonic Scale

The Open-Position D Minor Pentatonic Scale

By eliminating the 2nd and 6th notes of our D minor scale from Chapter 7, we get the D minor pentatonic scale, which contains the same notes as the relative F major pentatonic scale.

D Minor Pentatonic Scale

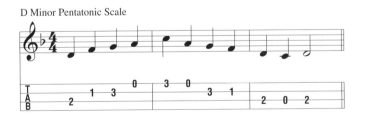

OPEN-POSITION MINOR PENTATONIC LICKS

Now let's try our hand at a few minor pentatonic licks in open position. Again, the minor pentatonic scale forms here look just like their relative major counterparts; the difference will be in the phrasing and how we resolve the licks.

A Minor Pentatonic Licks

First, we'll work with the A minor pentatonic scale. Again, notice how we're ending our phrases on the A note.

This is not to say that you always have to end your licks on A if you're playing an A minor pentatonic scale; that's not the case at all. But with no other context (i.e., no bass note or backing chord), ending on A is sure to convey the minor pentatonic sound as opposed to C major pentatonic.

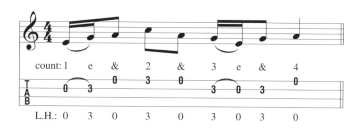

In this next example, look at the last two notes: The open third string and the open first string. Although you could allow both strings to ring and it will still sound harmonious, it will sound more final if you mute the third string as you play the first string. In other words, if you're plucking the notes with your thumb, then after you pluck the open third string on beat 4, you can touch it with the thumb (to deaden it) as you pluck the open first string with the index or middle finger. This is the way the lick is performed on the audio track.

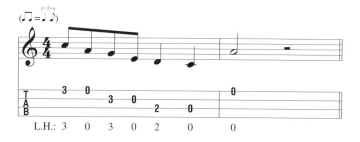

Here's a good example of how you can recycle the material of one lick to create another. Notice that the notes here are exactly the same as those in the lick from Track 66. The only thing that's changed is the rhythm.

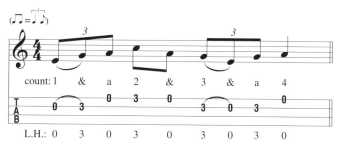

D Minor Pentatonic Licks

Now let's work from the D minor pentatonic scale.

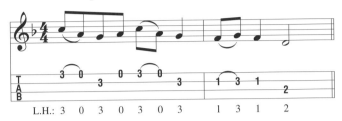

In this next lick, we're recycling the rhythm from the A minor pentatonic lick of Track 68, but we're changing the notes to make it fit D minor pentatonic.

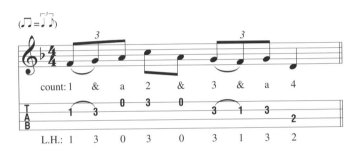

Of course, not all songs are in 4/4, so here's a lick in 3/4 played with a shuffle feel.

MOVEABLE MAJOR PENTATONIC SCALE FORMS

We can create moveable scale forms the same way we created barre chord forms: We re-finger the open versions using the "zero fret" approach.

Moveable Major Pentatonic Form 1

Our first moveable major pentatonic form will be based off our open C major pentatonic scale. So let's re-finger that scale by using our first finger behind the nut for all the open-string notes. Pay close attention to the L.H. fingering under the tab.

C Major Pentatonic

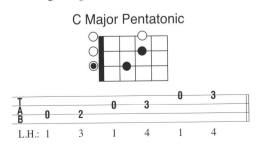

Now, just move everything up one fret, and we get a D♭ major pentatonic scale.

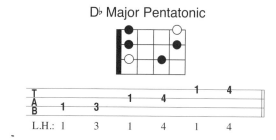

So, your first moveable major pentatonic form, which begins and ends on the tonic, looks like this:

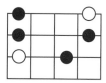

Moveable Major Pentatonic Form 2

Our second form will be based off the open F major pentatonic scale, which has the tonic on string 2. After performing the same procedure as above, we end up with this:

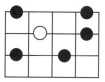

EXTENDED MAJOR PENTATONIC FORMS

We can extend the range of each of these forms by shifting up in position slightly.

Extended Major Pentatonic Form 1

If we take Form 1 and move the lowest note on string 2 over to string 3, and the lowest note on string 1 to string 2, we can reach one note higher on top.

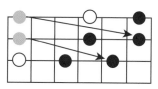

So we end up with this:

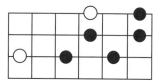

Extended Major Pentatonic Form 2

Likewise, we can do a similar move with Form 2:

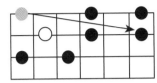

And we end up with this:

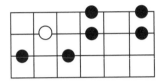

Slides

But the benefit of these extended forms isn't merely to gain access to a higher note; it also affords the use of a great phrasing tool called the *slide*. Similar to hammer-ons and pull-offs, the slide is a legato technique that provides a smooth connection between two notes.

It's fairly self-explanatory: You simply play one note and then slide your finger up or down to a target note, maintaining fretboard pressure throughout. In the music, slides are notated with a *gliss* symbol, or a diagonal line.

There are basically three types of slide: *slurred*, *plucked*, and *decorative*. The slurred slide is the most common, so we'll start there.

The Slurred Slide

To perform this move, simply pluck a note and slide to another note on the same string without plucking again, being sure to maintain pressure along the way. In the music, you'll see the slide symbol (diagonal line) with a slur.

Slurred slides are generally used for notes that move fairly quickly because, if you don't slide soon enough after you pluck the note, you won't hear the slide.

The Plucked Slide

For the plucked slide, you do the same thing, but you pluck both the starting note and the target note. This is indicated in the music by the slide symbol without the slur.

The Decorative Slide

This is more of an ornament and doesn't really have any rhythmic value. If the slide is a specific distance, it's notated with a *grace note*—a small note preceding the main note—and a slur. The grace note occupies no real time value; it's just a note played *en route* to the main note. The audio track will make it clear.

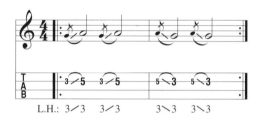

If the slide is a non-specific distance, then you'll just see the slide symbol before or after the note, and it's left up to the performer to determine how far the slide should be.

You can also use the decorative slide for a *fall-off*, which is an indeterminate slide down or up the fretboard at the *end* of the note. This is indicated by the slide symbol after the note.

Although these slide techniques certainly sound interesting, they, like everything, are best used in moderation. If you start throwing in slides every which way, on every other note, they'll start to lose their effectiveness.

EXTENDED MAJOR PENTATONIC FORM LICKS

Now let's put these slides to use in some licks from our extended major pentatonic forms.

Extended Major Pentatonic Form 1 Licks

First, let's play some licks from Form 1.

> The tonic on this scale form lies at the bottom of the form, on string 3. By using your Fretboard Map for string 3 (page 42), you can move the form around to play licks in different keys.

This first one is in D major. Note that the L.H. fingering here is just a suggestion. Some people prefer to slide on string 3 with their middle finger, and some prefer their ring finger. Sometimes the context will dictate which makes more sense.

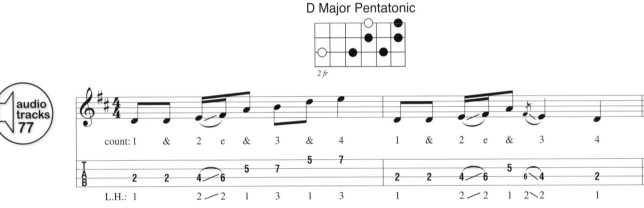

Here's one in F major that's a lot of fun. We've got some syncopation (the "and" of beat 2) and staccato markings in measure 1 that really make it come alive.

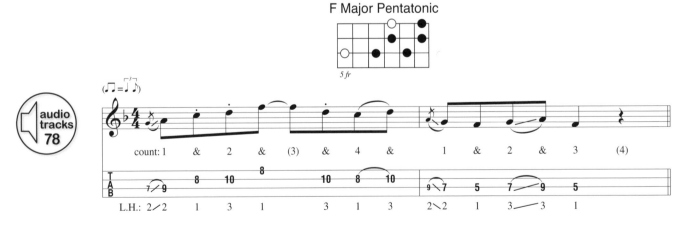

Extended Major Pentatonic Form 2 Licks

Now it's time for Form 2. Remember that the tonic lies on string 2 in this form. This first one is in G major.

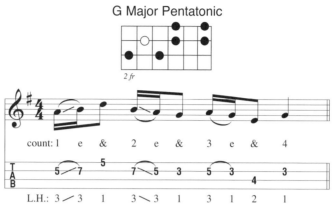

Here's a lick in 6/8 meter from the B♭ major pentatonic scale. Notice the *rhythmic imitation* of measures 1 and 2—another great phrasing device.

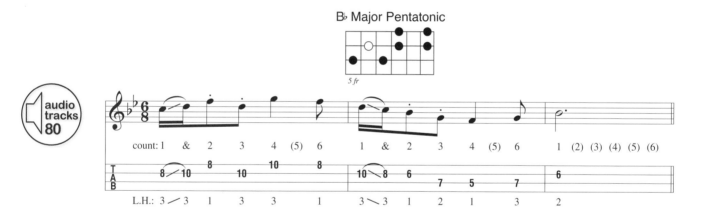

MOVEABLE MINOR PENTATONIC SCALE FORMS

Now let's check out some moveable minor pentatonic scale forms. We'll add the extended form to each as well.

Moveable Minor Pentatonic Form 1

This first form will be based off the open A minor pentatonic form. The tonic is on string 1 in this form. Using the same "zero fret" procedure as before, the form will look like this:

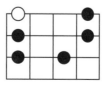

Extended Minor Pentatonic Form 1

By moving notes to lower strings and shifting up the fretboard, we get the extended version of Form 1. Note that the tonic has been moved to string 2.

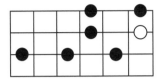

Remember that the tonic in every scale form is represented by an open circle. To play the scale in any key, simply slide the form up or down until the tonic note is in place.

Moveable Minor Pentatonic Form 2

This form is based off the open D minor form. The tonic is on string 3 here.

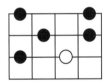

Extended Minor Pentatonic Form 2

The extended form gives us access to two tonic notes, top and bottom.

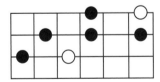

MOVEABLE MINOR PENTATONIC FORM LICKS

Now let's play some minor pentatonic licks with our moveable and extended forms. We'll identify the key and scale form for each lick.

In this first lick, from B minor pentatonic, you'll "roll" your index finger from string 1 to string 2 on beat 1. In other words, when you're preparing for the pull-off from fret 5 on string 1, use the pad of your index finger on fret 2 instead of the tip. This will allow you to roll over to your tip on string 2. Similarly, at the very end, roll from the tip of your index finger on string 3 to the pad on string 1.

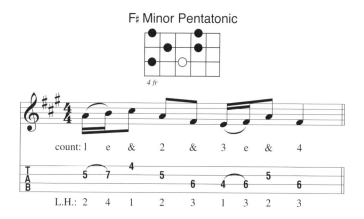

If hammering from your middle finger to your pinky, as is shown in the L.H. fingering for the previous lick, is too difficult at this point, you can use your index and ring finger instead, shifting back to fret 4 with your index finger afterwards for the note on string 1.

Here's one in 6/8 from the C minor pentatonic extended form. Note the "let ring" indication at the beginning; this tells you to allow the notes contained within the span of the dashed line to ring together, as in a chord. In the second half of measure 1, you'll roll your ring finger from tip (string 2) to pad (string 1) and back again.

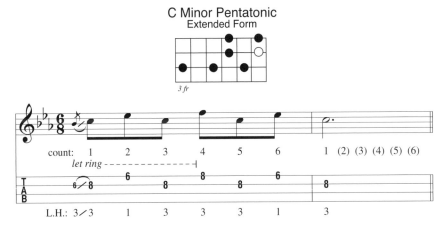

And we'll close out here with a real doozie from the extended G minor pentatonic form. What makes this one so special, aside from the numerous slides and pull-offs, is the syncopation on beat 4. We're playing four 16th notes and then sustaining the last one over the bar line until the "and" of beat 1. Watch the count very closely and be sure to check the audio track to make sure you have the rhythm right.

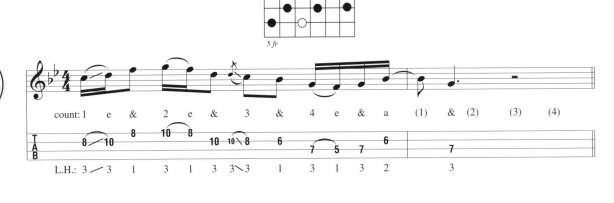

- The major pentatonic scale is a five-note version of the major scale with the 4th and 7th notes omitted.
- The minor pentatonic scale is a five-note version of the minor scale with the 2nd and 6th notes omitted.
- The open-position C major pentatonic and F major pentatonic scales form the basis for two moveable major pentatonic forms.
- The open-position A minor pentatonic and D minor pentatonic scales form the basis for two moveable minor pentatonic forms.
- When playing two notes on adjacent strings at the same fret, you can "roll" your finger from one string to the next.
- Hammer-ons, pull-offs, and slides provide a smooth, connected legato sound and can also allow you to play certain licks at faster tempos.

CHAPTER 11
FUN WITH FINGERPICKING

What's Ahead:
- What's an arpeggio
- Basic fingerpicking patterns
- Alternating-thumb fingerpicking patterns
- Block chord "piano-style" fingerpicking
- Chord-changing strategies for smooth transitions
- Decorating your fingerpicking patterns with hammer-ons, pull-offs, and slides

---

Now it's time to enter the exciting world of fingerpicking. This technique can greatly expand your ukulele horizons, opening vast new worlds of musical expression—not to mention it's really fun! There are many different types of fingerpicking styles, and in this chapter, we'll chow down on the sampler platter.

WHAT'S AN ARPEGGIO?

We've been playing chords by strumming them, essentially attacking all of the notes at once, whereas an *arpeggio* is a chord that's played one note at a time, in succession. You know how we said it's a good idea to pluck the strings of a new chord individually to make sure you're playing it cleanly? Well, that was an arpeggio. With the fingerpicking technique, however, we'll be using our thumb and fingers to pluck the strings—not just brushing the thumb through the strings one at a time.

BASIC ARPEGGIOS 101

Let's get started with some simple arpeggios to get your fingers acquainted with the technique. First, plant your thumb, index, middle, and ring fingers on strings 4–1, respectively. Your thumb should be slightly ahead (i.e., closer to the nut) of your index finger. Although we usually strum just over the end of the fretboard, we usually fingerpick over the soundhole so that the fretboard doesn't interfere with our plucking.

Once you're in position, grab an open G chord and pluck through the strings in order, from thumb to ring finger. When identifying the fingers of the right hand, we'll use the same abbreviations that classical guitarists use: *p* = thumb, *i* = index, *m* = middle, and *a* = ring (these come from the archaic Spanish words *pulgar*, *indicio*, *medular*, and *anular*).

Notice that, due to the reentrant tuning, the notes are a bit jumbled. In other words, they don't simply rise and fall as they would on a guitar, for example. This is one of the things that gives the ukulele its charm.

Now try plucking up and down through the strings in a 3/4 pattern. At this point, your fingers, after plucking, should be just hovering above the strings so that all the strings are allowed to ring completely.

Just as with your fretting hand, your right-hand fingertips are likely going to get a bit sore when you start fingerpicking. However, you'll develop calluses on them as well, and the pain will shortly subside.

Some players choose to grow out their fingernails for fingerpicking, while others keep them trimmed short. This is entirely a personal preference. Playing with nails will produce a brighter, crisper sound; fingers will produce a warmer, darker tone. If you do choose to grow your nails, keep in mind that you'll need to maintain them by filing them occasionally. Many people apply nail hardener to help prevent breakage.

Next, let's try our ascending pattern again, but this time moving from a G chord to a C chord. We'll play two measures of a G chord and then we'll replant all of our fingers and thumb before starting the C chord. Try to make this sound as seamless as possible. In other words, you want to be plucking with the thumb on beat 1 of the C chord just as your *i*, *m*, and *a* fingers plant on their strings. Do this replanting before each new chord.

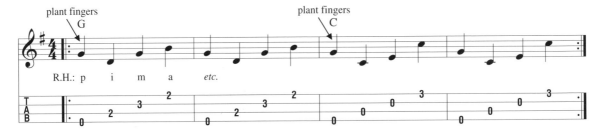

You don't have to replant your fingers for each new chord; it just makes for a clean sound. Try playing the previous example again but leave your fingers floating the entire time to hear the difference. You'll probably notice the sound of some of your fingers fretting notes of the G chord before you pluck them, or you may hear your fingers lifting off the G chord in preparation for the C chord.

This is somewhat of a subtle thing, but it's a good idea to get into the habit of planting your fingers early on because you'll then have a choice. It's always easy to keep the fingers floating, so you'll have that option at your disposal. In other fingerpicking techniques, we won't be planting the fingers at all; we'll keep them floating throughout. But these simple ascending and descending arpeggios work well when planting is implemented.

And now try the same thing only in a descending pattern: *a–m–i–p.*

Next is an example in the key of A that moves between an A chord, a D chord, and a new chord called Eadd4. It sounds fancy, but all you're doing is simply moving the fretted notes of the D chord up two frets while keeping string 1 open.

Since the open first string is common to all three chords, it sounds nice to let it ring throughout. Experiment with planting the fingers for each chord and then allowing them to float throughout to see which you like better. We're increasing the speed a little here by using eighth notes.

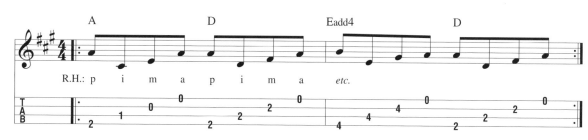

If you choose to not plant the fingers, try being as quiet as you can when fretting the chords so you don't create extra noise. One method for this is basically "fretting as you go." In other words, don't fret a note until you need to pluck it.

EASY ARPEGGIO SONGS

Let's try playing some songs with these arpeggio patterns. Our first is the old English ballad "Scarborough Fair." This one is in 3/4 and uses the rolling pattern from Track 86.

Scarborough Fair

Traditional English

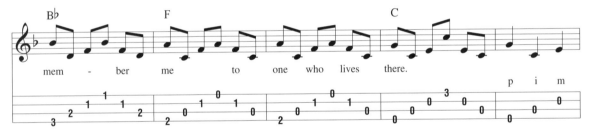

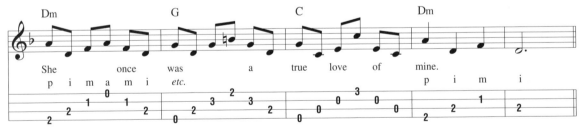

This famous song about a town in Yorkshire, England called Scarborough most likely dates back to 1670 or earlier. It features a melody from the Dorian mode, which is like a minor scale but with a raised 6th tone. (Notice the B natural accidental in the G major chord; this is because we normally have a B♭ in the key of D minor.) The Dorian mode is very common in English folk songs.

Next, let's pluck our way through Radiohead's "Karma Police," which is in 4/4. For most of the song, we'll use our ascending *p–i–m–a* pattern, but we'll alter it in the chorus just a bit, coming back down on the F♯ chord to imitate the song's arpeggio pattern at that time.

Karma Police

Words and Music by Thomas Yorke, Jonathan Greenwood,
Colin Greenwood, Edward O'Brien and Philip Selway

Additional lyrics:
2. Karma police, arrest this girl.
   Her Hitler hairdo is making me feel ill.
   And we have crashed her party.

ALTERNATING-THUMB PATTERNS

Let's continue on now with some *alternating-thumb patterns*. With this style, the thumb will alternate between strings 4 and 3 (or 3 and 4) while the *i* and *m* fingers will pluck upbeat notes on strings 2 and 1, respectively. If you've ever heard the term "Travis picking" with regard to guitar, this is kind of the ukulele version of that.

The term "Travis picking" comes from one of the pioneers of the guitar technique—country legend Merle Travis. His thumb (he wore a thumbpick, actually) would alternate between a low bass note and a mid-register chord fragment while his index finger was used to fill in the gaps on top. Now the term has been applied to basically any fingerpicking pattern in which the thumb is alternating between strings while the fingers add notes on top.

4-3 Thumb Pattern

Let's start with a basic exercise in which we simply alternate the thumb between strings 4 and 3 in quarter notes. It looks like this:

Once you've got that down, add the *i* finger on string 2 and the *a* finger on string 1 in the gaps. With a C chord, it will sound like this:

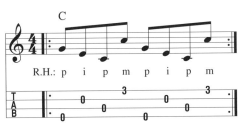

Again, the reentrant tuning makes this pattern sound much different than if it were played on a guitar but, again, that's what makes the uke unique. Let's try moving between a C chord and an F chord.

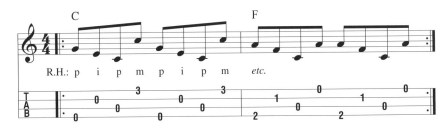

Chord-Changing Strategies

Moving from C to F poses no real problems with regard to changing chords because no fingers have to quickly leap somewhere. However, take a look at what happens when you move from G to F.

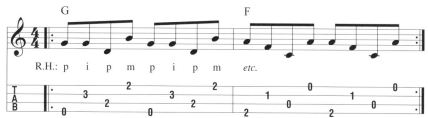

Do you see the issue? After the last note of the G chord—the B note on fret 2, string 1—your left-hand middle finger has to leap down to string 4, fret 2 in the space of an eighth note. It's the last note in one measure and the first note in the next. Needless to say, it's difficult to pull this off. It's not impossible to make it sound acceptable with practice, but it's certainly not a walk in the park. However, with some creative thinking, there are ways to get around it.

Strategy 1: Use an Open String if Possible

The first method is similar to the open-string cheat we talked about with strumming. If the open first string happens to be in the key of the song and doesn't sound bad, you can simply lift the fretting finger off at that point and pluck the open string, giving that fret-hand finger time to get into position for the next downbeat.

In our case, the open A string will sound just fine, so that's an option. It would sound like this:

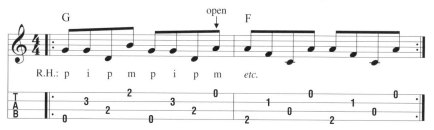

Strategy 2: Use an Alternate Chord Fingering

Another possibility is to see if there's an alternate way to fret one of the chords. In our case, we could fret the G chord with the middle, ring, and pinky. This would mean that the last note of the G chord is fretted with the ring finger. Therefore, the middle finger could start moving early and make the change in time.

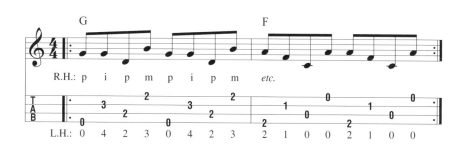

Strategy 3: Omit the Final Note of the Measure

If neither of the previous two options are a possibility, then you can always simply omit the final eighth note of the measure. In other words, you would just end the measure with a quarter note played by the thumb. In our case, that would sound like this.

This option will usually work just fine, especially at faster tempos.

When fingerpicking, remember that you don't have to fret the whole chord right on the downbeat. Since the notes of the chord are typically played in succession, you'll get an extra split second to change fingerings if needed. For example, when moving from G to F, the only note that needs to be present on the downbeat of the F chord is the A note on string 4, fret 2 (fretted with the middle finger). You have an extra split second to place the index finger for the F note on string 2, fret 1. Likewise, when moving from F to G, the first note of the G chord (in this pattern) is the open fourth string. So the chord doesn't actually require full fretting until the "and" of beat 1.

Alternate 4-3 Thumb Pattern

Of course, we have one more option with the 4–3 thumb pattern, and that's to reverse the order of the fingers. So, instead of *p–i–p–m*, we'd play *p–m–p–i*. On a C chord, it sounds like this:

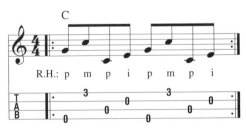

Note that this is essentially the opposite of our *p–i–p–m* pattern. Whereas that one created a descending cascade on our C chord, this pattern creates an ascending cascade.

Let's try it out on a progression in D major. We'll be using a shuffle feel on this one, which sounds great with fingerpicking. For a bit of variation, we're omitting the very last note in measure 4.

Different chord voicings will produce different effects with these patterns, which is always interesting. Here is a nice-sounding progression that moves from an open Em to a Bm7 barre chord.

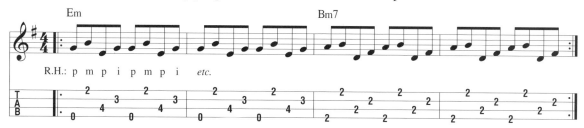

3-4 Thumb Pattern

Now let's take a look at the other thumb pattern, in which we'll alternate between string 3 and 4. On a C chord, the standard pattern would look like this:

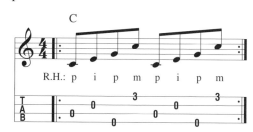

Notice that it runs straight up a C chord in pitch, from low to high. With other chords, it may slightly change, but the lowest-sounding note of the chord voicing will always appear at the beginning of the measure with this pattern, which is nice to know.

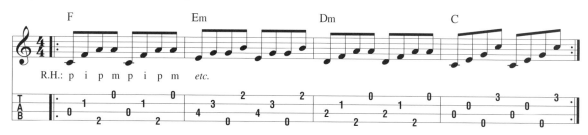

Alternate 3-4 Thumb Pattern

Finally, we can reverse the finger notes on this pattern as well, giving us the *p–m–p–i* pattern. On a C chord, that will sound like this:

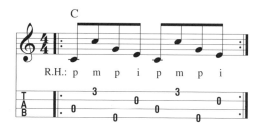

Here's another shuffle-feel example, this time moving between Em7 and Am7:

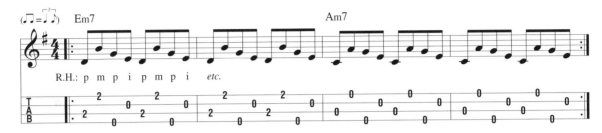

ALTERNATING-THUMB PATTERN VARIATIONS

We can add even more variation to these patterns as well. Let's look at two ways here…

Plucking Simultaneous Notes

The first method is to play one or more of the finger-plucked notes on the beat *with* the thumb note, instead of in between the thumb notes. This is sometimes called "pinching." It's very common to play a pinch on beat 1, for example. Here's an example of this idea that alternates between G and C chords. We're using a *p–m–p–i* pattern, but the first *m* note of each measure is pinched with the thumb.

For the following figure, if you use the middle finger of your left hand on string 1 for the C chord, you'll avoid an awkward move when coming from G. This way, the middle finger can stay on string 1 and just slide up and down a fret.

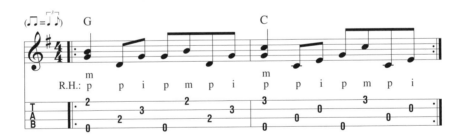

If you're having trouble making a chord change sound smooth, try one of the "Chord-Changing Strategies" from page 105. Chances are, one of the three methods will do the trick.

The possibilities really grow when you combine this idea with different patterns. Here's a beautiful progression in F major that uses a *p–i–p–m* pattern with a pinch on beat 1.

Adding Hammer-Ons, Pull-Offs, or Slides

You can decorate your patterns even further by adding hammer-ons or pull-offs to your pinched notes. Let's look at some examples of that.

Let's start with a shuffle pattern that alternates between G and Cmaj7 chords. We're using a *p–m–p–i* pattern with a pinch on beat 1 and just a quarter note on beat 4. It looks like this:

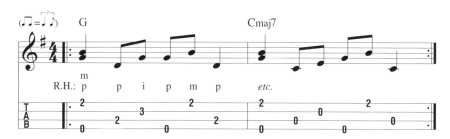

But now listen to what it sounds like when we hammer onto that fret 2 note on string 1 at the beginning of each measure. The pattern really comes alive! Notice that the right hand is playing the exact same thing, but the hammer-ons make it sound much more sophisticated.

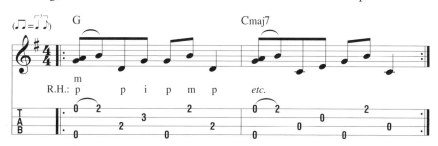

Here's another example, this time using pull-offs and moving from Em7 to Am7:

And next we'll look at an idea using slides. First, we're sliding into the G major chord from a half step below. Then, we're sliding up a whole step to a new voicing of Am7, which looks like this:

Am7

Notice that both chords use the open fourth string. Also, both slides occur on a pinch with the thumb and *i* finger, so you can fret the rest of the chord after the slide in each case.

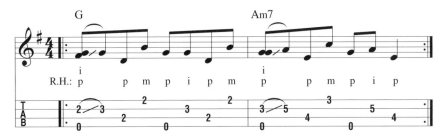

ALTERNATING-THUMB-PATTERN SONGS

OK, now let's put these patterns to use in some songs. We'll see how these patterns can be combined and/or varied to serve the necessary textures for each piece.

First up is Shawn Colvin's mid-'90s folk-rock hit "Sunny Came Home." We'll play this one in G minor and use a modified alternating-thumb pattern to play a fairly convincing facsimile of the intro. Then we'll move into more of a standard pattern for the verse and chorus, albeit with a pinch on beat 1 and an omitted note on beat 4. Note the new chord that appears in the verse:

Sunny Came Home

Words and Music by Shawn Colvin and John Leventhal

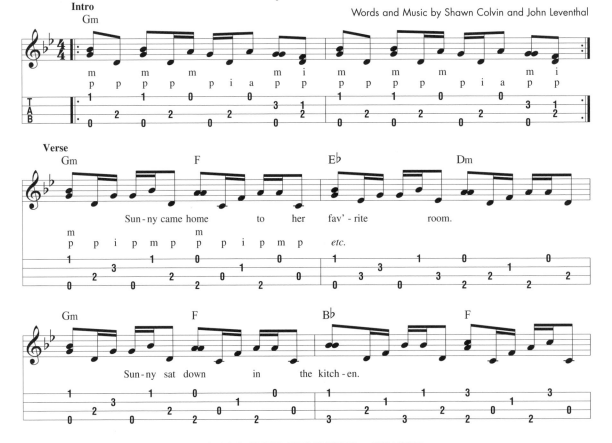

And here's yet another female folk-rock ditty from the '90s: Jewel's breakout hit "Who Will Save Your Soul." This one's in A minor and has a shuffle feel. The chord progression here is pretty repetitive, so we'll try to liven it up by decorating the chords in a manner similar to the original guitar part. Having said that, here are two new chords, both of which are very easy:

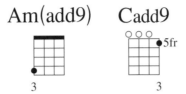

The fingerpicking pattern here is slightly different as well. We're alternating the thumb in a 4–3 pattern and we're pinching on beat 1 with the *m* finger, but then we're playing on the "and" of beat 1 with the *i* finger, too. Basically, it's just like the *p–i–p–m* pattern but with an added *m* pinch on beat 1. We're also omitting the final eighth note in each measure.

Who Will Save Your Soul

Words and Music by Jewel Murray

And now let's play one more for good measure. "Can't Find My Way Home" is a signature song of the short-lived '70s supergroup Blind Faith, featuring Steve Winwood, Eric Clapton, Ginger Baker, and Ric Grech. The chord progression has a hypnotic quality that just keeps pulling you in, over and over. We'll play it here in the key of A, using a nearly unbroken *p–i–p–m* pattern. Notice that we occasionally employ the open-string cheat—particularly at the end of the G chords—in order to keep the momentum flowing.

At the end of the chorus, we quickly move through two chord shapes to imply the descending movement. Both feature notes on strings 4 and 3, with strings 2 and 1 open on top:

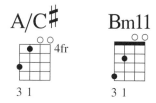

Can't Find My Way Home

Words and Music by Steve Winwood

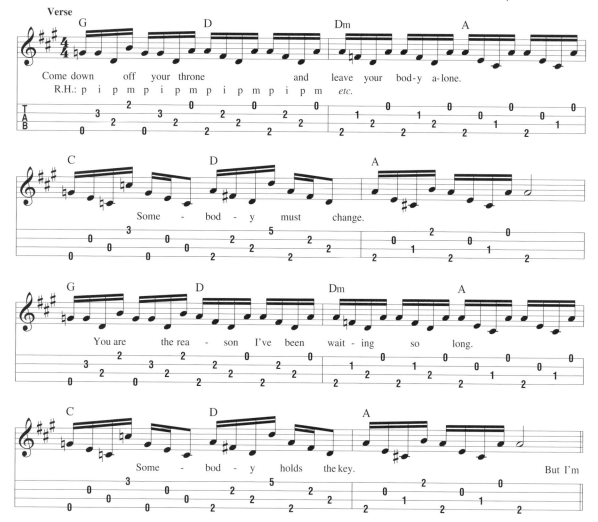

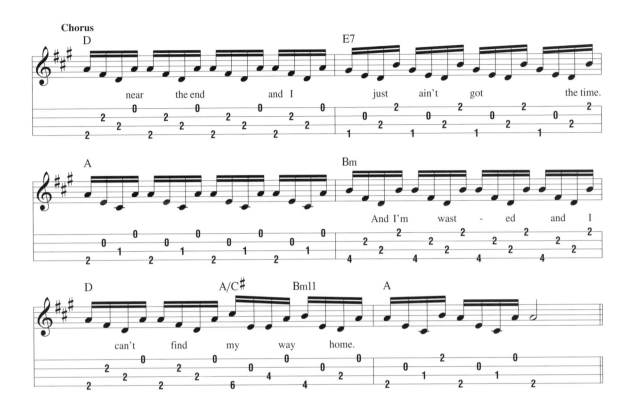

Chorus

D — near the end and I

E7 — just ain't got the time.

A — And I'm wast - ed and I

Bm

D — can't find my way home.

A/C♯   Bm11   A

try this

Just as with strumming patterns, these fingerpicking patterns aren't carved in stone. Once you get these down, feel free to mix it up a bit if you'd like. For example, try playing a song with a 3-4 thumb pattern instead of a 4-3 pattern. This can not only keep things interesting, but it can also lead to new discoveries or other "happy accidents."

BLOCK-CHORD STYLE

The final technique we'll look at is the block-chord style—sometimes called the "piano style." With this technique, you use your thumb and fingers to pluck the strings simultaneously instead of one at a time. In this way, it's kind of similar to strumming, but the sound is quite different, as are the types of rhythms we play.

To get acquainted with the idea, try plucking all four strings of a C chord and a G chord.

audio tracks 109

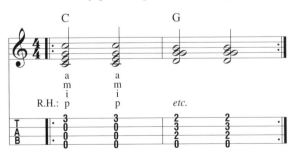

The sound is somewhat piano-like, as it simulates the way a pianist might play a chord.

Make sure that you're clearly hearing every note in the chord. This will take a bit of practice, as the sound will most likely be a bit lopsided at first (the thumb will be quieter or louder than the other fingers, etc.). Start by alternating between plucking the strings individually and then simultaneously to make sure all the notes are present.

Once you add a bit of syncopation, you can start to get some nice grooves. Here, we're moving between Dm7 and G7, adding a rest and accenting the "and" of beat 2.

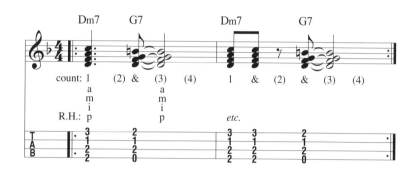

Separating the Thumb and Fingers

For a variation, you can separate the thumb and fingers. For example, you could pluck with the thumb on the "and" before the chord and then play the chord on the beat with the fingers. You might come up with something like this:

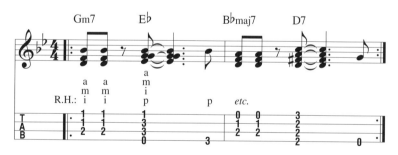

Or you could put the fingers on the downbeats and the thumb on the upbeats, like this:

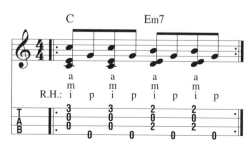

Adding a Percussive Backbeat

This is a great way to get a groove going. It's basically the same idea as some of our earlier examples in this section, but on beats 2 and 4, you forcefully plant your fingers onto the strings to create a percussive "smack." It sounds reminiscent of a snare drum, so it really grooves.

Here's the basic idea, moving from A to D7:

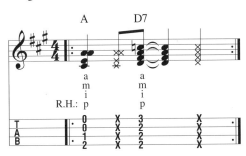

By separating the thumb and fingers a bit, we can make this one really groove:

Here's another take on the idea, this time with a progression in A minor:

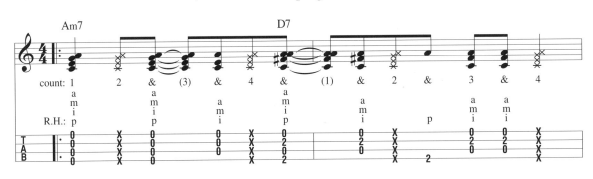

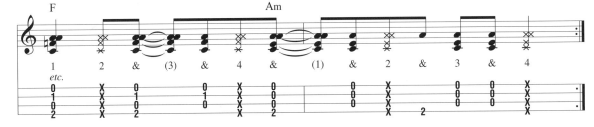

As you can hear, you can really create a one-man-band feel with this technique. Just add some vocals, and you've got a show!

BLOCK-CHORD-STYLE SONGS

Let's wrap up this chapter with a few songs that use the block-chord style. First up is Aerosmith's classic anthem "Dream On." This one illustrates an important point about the block-chord style: Who says you have to use all four strings? The classic riff here makes use of three-note chords only, with the index finger and middle finger on strings 2 and 1, respectively, alternating with the thumb on string 3. We'll play this one in A minor. A few of these chords will be new, but don't worry about that yet; just follow the tablature, and you'll be in good shape.

Dream On

Words and Music by Steven Tyler

Next, we'll take a look at Extreme's "More Than Words." This song is a classic example of the percussive backbeat technique. Though it was played on guitar on the original recording, we can generate a great-sounding arrangement in the key of C on the uke.

There are two new chord forms here to note. First is an Fadd9. Simply play an E♭ chord but slide all the fretted notes up two frets, keeping the open fourth string. The other is an alternate voicing for a C chord.

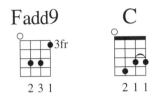

More Than Words

Words and Music by Nuno Bettencourt and Gary Cherone

Finally, we'll wrap up with the Beatles' "Let It Be." As we mentioned earlier, the block-chord style is sometimes called the piano style, and this is a case in point, as we're going to be imitating Paul McCartney's piano part. For the most part, we're playing fingers on the beat and thumb on the upbeat, but there are a few little exceptions here and there. Keep an eye on the tab to clear up any confusion.

Let It Be

Words and Music by John Lennon and Paul McCartney

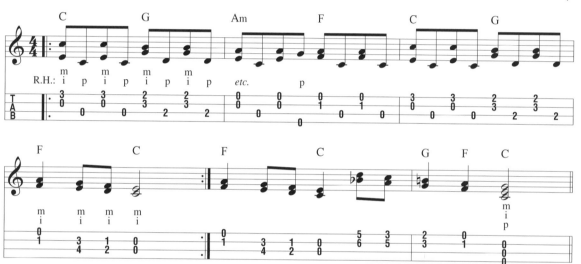

- There are three main fingerpicking approaches: Arpeggios, alternating-thumb patterns, and block-chord style.
- The right-hand fingers are indicated as follows: p = thumb, i = index, m = middle, a = ring.
- You can use pinches, hammer-ons, pull-offs, and slides to decorate your fingerpicking patterns.
- There are three strategies for smoothing out a tough chord change: 1) use an open string (if possible), 2) use an alternate chord fingering, or 3) omit the last eighth note of the measure.

CHAPTER 12

MORE STRUMMING VARIATIONS

What's Ahead:

- More sophisticated strum rhythms
- The power of accents
- 16th-note and triplet syncopations
- Adding muted strums
- Alternate strum patterns for triplets

Now let's return to the world of strumming and expand our options a bit. In this chapter, we'll pick up where we left off, adding more rests, more syncopation, and other textures to our strumming vocabulary. By the end of this chapter, you'll be armed with lots of applicable "real world" techniques employed in songs of all genres.

ADDING ACCENTS TO YOUR STRUMMING PATTERNS

We've briefly mentioned the concept of accents earlier in the book, but now we're going to look at them more deliberately. Though the concept is often overlooked by many, changing the accents of a strum pattern—both dynamically and rhythmically—can have a dramatic effect on the music. It's another subtlety of music (much like the use of staccato) that can really bring something to life.

Dynamic Accents

The first type of accent we'll look at is the *dynamic* accent. This has to do predominantly with volume. In other words, we're going to strum certain chords quieter and others louder to accent them. But we'll also incorporate staccato into this as well, because the two concepts often work hand in hand. To illustrate, let's play a few examples in a comparative fashion, in which we use all the same notes but vary how they're played.

First up is a common progression in C major: I–vi–ii–V (C–Am–Dm7–G7). We'll play it with all moveable chord shapes, around third position.

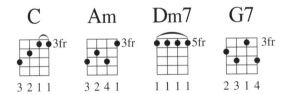

Roman numerals like this refer to the scale degree on which each chord is built. In this case, by numbering the C major scale as C(1)–D(2)–E(3)–F(4)–G(5)–A(6)–B(7), we can see the correlation. C(1) = I, A(6) = vi, D(2) = ii, and G(5) = V. Uppercase Roman numerals indicate major chords, while lowercase numerals indicate minor chords.

Often, Roman numerals will only indicate the triad function, but occasionally you'll see sevenths added as well. So, you may also see this progression presented as I–vi–ii7–V7.

First, we'll play it in straight quarter notes with no special articulations.

Version A

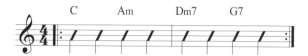

OK, so it's a nice-sounding progression that flows well. There's nothing particularly wrong with this, but it's a bit bland. Let's try it again but with each chord played staccato. Since these are moveable chord forms, with no open strings, you only need to slightly release the fret-hand pressure after strumming to create the staccato effect.

Version B

We can already hear how it has more bounce and life to it; it starts to sound like music. Let's try another variation now. This time, we'll play long, quieter strums on beats 1 and 3 and accented (louder) staccato strums on beats 2 and 4.

Version C

Now we're talking! The pattern breathes in a very musical way. Let's try one more quick example. We'll start with a gentle shuffling pattern in eighth notes, alternating between F#m7 and B7. Here are the chord forms:

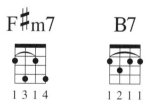

And here's the pattern:

Version A

That sounded nice, and there's nothing wrong with it at all. But it could sound a bit more dynamic by adding some accents.

Version B

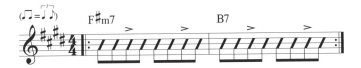

By making beats 2 and 4 staccato, it gets even more dynamic.

Version C

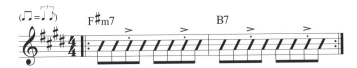

Again, this is not to say that versions B and C will always sound better than version A. There are times when an understated, even sound will fit the bill better. The point is to illustrate what options you have available when you want them.

Rhythmic Accents with Syncopation

Now we'll turn to the other side of the accent coin: Rhythmic syncopation. We've discussed syncopation previously but again, now we'll be a bit more deliberate and systematic with it. This is another factor that can turn four unassuming chords into a serious groove.

We'll use a nice four-bar progression in C major as our playing field. The chords will be C–Am7–Fadd9–G+. Here are the chord forms:

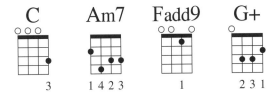

The "+" suffix in G+ stands for *augmented*. An augmented chord is another kind of triad. It's like a major triad but with a raised (or sharped) 5th. So, whereas a G major triad is spelled G(root)–B(3rd)–D(5th), a G augmented triad is spelled G(root)–B(3rd)–D#(#5th).

This chord is non-diatonic to the major scale, which means it doesn't occur naturally within the key signature. This is why the sound of it will stick out compared to the other three; it creates more tension that needs to be resolved.

Below is the original pattern, which contains nothing but eighth notes, with two beats for each chord. Note that, even though these are eighth notes, you could strum this with all downstrokes because of the slow tempo.

So these are some nice voicings, and they create a lovely-sounding progression. But now let's apply some rhythmic accents via syncopation. The first thing we're going to do is shift the Am7 and G+ chords one eighth note earlier (i.e., to the left). That will sound like this:

Notice how this already gooses the pattern quite a bit with forward momentum. Next, let's add a tie after those anticipated chords to really set them apart. To further highlight the effect, we'll slide into them from a half step below. Tab notation is provided so you can clearly see what's happening.

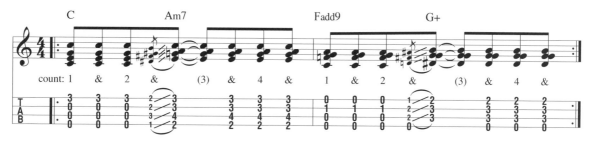

If sliding into the Am7 chord is difficult, try out this method: Rather than worrying about the slide, simply play the starting chord a half step below for now. In other words, play the C chord for three eighth notes and then play the G#m7 chord in first position (i.e., the chord in tab that's to the left of the diagonal lines). Once you can solidly play that chord in time, then start working on sliding it up one fret to the target Am7 chord.

Now it's really coming to life! Let's add some 16th-note strums to busy it up a bit more. At this point, if you hadn't already, you'll want to move to downstrokes on the eighth notes throughout. Pay close attention to the strum indications, as this is the first time you're encountering a 16th-note syncopation. Again, your right hand needs to be the steady time-keeper here. Keep the hand moving down with every eighth note and only connect with the upstrokes when needed.

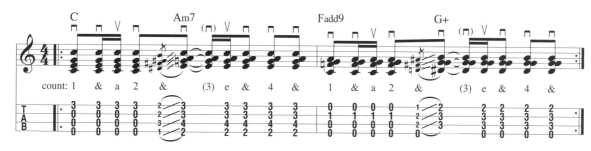

Wow! Take a second to go back to the first example (Track 122) to hear how far we've come. It's quite a different animal at this point. Let's take it even further with one last adjustment. We'll add yet another 16th-note syncopation by incorporating a tie at the end of beat 1 and a 16th-note strum on the "e" of beat 2. Again, keep the right hand moving in a steady stream of downstrokes for every eighth note.

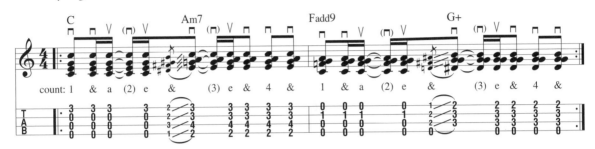

As you can see, you can take this kind of thing quite far and get as sophisticated as you like.

Just as with the accents, we're not implying that more syncopation is always better. Sometimes a set of straight eighth notes is just what the song needs, but it's good to be able to funk it up a bit when you want to!

ADDING MUTED STRUMS

Another very expressive strum technique is the use of *muted strums*, or *dead notes*. This is a very common sound on the guitar, especially in funk styles, but you'll hear it in all kinds of pop and rock songs too. We can use the same idea to great effect on the uke.

Start with a C-form D barre chord in second position. Strum it once and then release the pressure with your left hand so that you're still making contact with the strings but not the fretboard. Then strum again and you'll hear the dead strum, which will sound like a percussive click.

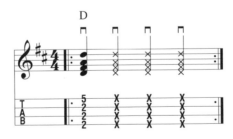

That's the basic idea. Now alternate strumming the D chord in quarter notes and the dead strums in eighth notes.

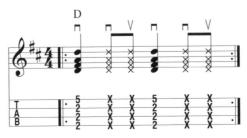

Let's turn that idea on its head.

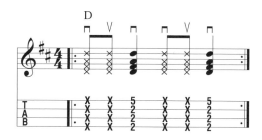

Fun, huh?! This idea works best with moveable chord forms because it's easier to mute all the strings when your left hand is already making contact with all of them.

Let's try a shuffle progression in B minor, using Bm, Em, and F#7 chords.

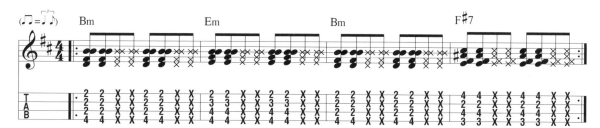

When you add some syncopation, it gets really fun. In this example, the right hand is strumming almost constant 16th notes throughout; the fret hand is responsible for sounding the chords by applying pressure at the appropriate times. We'll move back to using rhythm-slash notation at this point since you've got the idea.

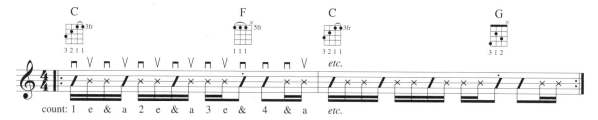

It's almost as if you can peck out a musical Morse code! Note the fingering shown for the following chords. When playing busier funky patterns like this, you may prefer this fingering instead of the barre fingering. Experiment and see what feels better.

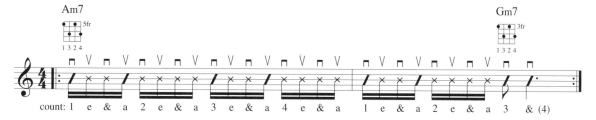

MUTED-STRUM SONGS

Let's check out how the muted-strum technique can be used in a couple of songs. First up is "Iz"'s (Israel Kamakawiwo'ole) beautiful version of "Somewhere over the Rainbow." Iz played a tenor uke with low G tuning for this song and used an interesting two-beat strum pattern. He played string 4 (which, remember, is a low bass note in low G tuning) with his thumb at the beginning of beat 1. Then, he strummed up-down-up in 16ths for the rest of the beat. On beat 2, he played a muted strum and then again, strummed up-down-up. He essentially repeats this two-beat pattern, with minor variation, throughout.

Over the Rainbow

from THE WIZARD OF OZ

Music by Harold Arlen
Lyric by E.Y. "Yip" Harburg

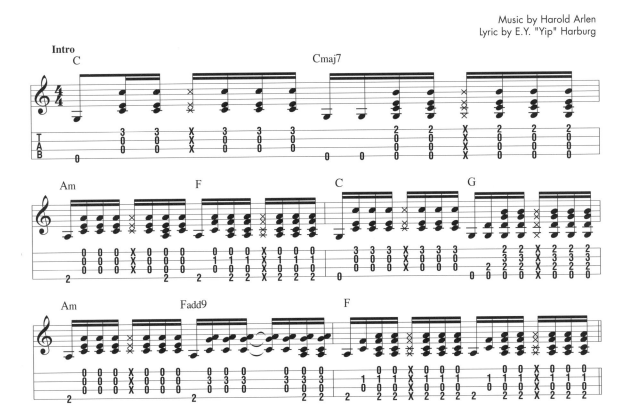

And now let's take a look at the Doobie Brothers' "China Grove." We'll adapt the signature opening guitar riff for uke, which greatly exploits the muted-strum effect.

China Grove

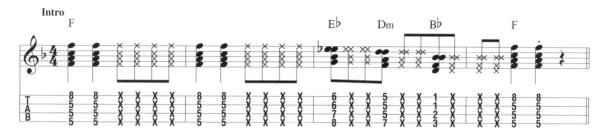

TRIPLET SYNCOPATION

We've talked a good bit about eighth- and 16th-note syncopation, but now we'll look at triplet syncopations. This means placing the accent on weak parts of a triplet beat.

To start with, let's play a two-chord progression, moving from G to Em7♭5 in straight triplets. Since the tempo is a bit faster this time, you'll most likely need to alternate down- and up-strums throughout.

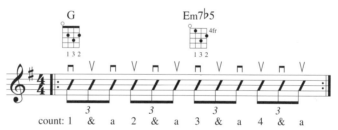

Now we'll play the same thing again, but we'll purposefully miss some downstrokes to accent a weak part of the beat. Watch the strum indications for the "missed" strums (shown in parentheses). First, we'll show it with ties to illustrate it better. Then, we'll show how it would normally be notated.

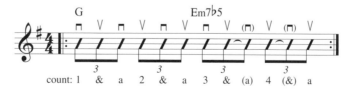

Sounds pretty fancy, huh? Here's a look at how it would usually be notated using triplet brackets:

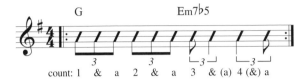

Or, if it were notated with a shuffle feel, it would look even simpler. Remember, the two eighth notes on beat 4 will sound just like the first and last notes of a triplet.

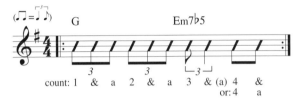

Some syncopation patterns will feel better when first strummed with an upstroke. Take a look at the following pattern, which adds muted strums to create the syncopation, and try both strumming indicators to see which feels better. When most people play this pattern, they tend to prefer starting with an upstroke. Remember to listen to the audio if the rhythm is too difficult to figure out.

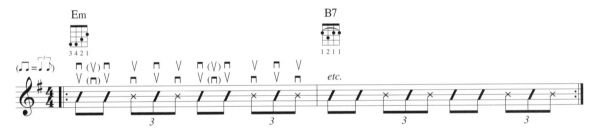

In order to hear some great examples of triplet syncopations, check out "Wall of Denial" by Stevie Ray Vaughan and "Higher Ground" by Stevie Wonder. (Seems that people named Stevie really like triplet syncopations!)

So, whereas 16th notes are more standardized—you're usually going to be pairing downstrums with the eighth notes—triplets aren't always so. You may have to experiment a bit to see which method feels and/or sounds best.

ALTERNATE STRUM PATTERNS FOR TRIPLETS

On that note, let's look at two other options for strumming continuous triplets. These will make use of more than one strumming finger.

Index-Thumb-Index

For our first method, we'll strum down with the index as normal. Then, we'll flick the thumb up to brush the strings with an upstroke. However, be sure to keep your index finger where it was after its downward strum. This is because we'll need it to finish the pattern with an upstrum. So, it's:

1.   Down with the index
2.   Up with the thumb
3.   Up with the index

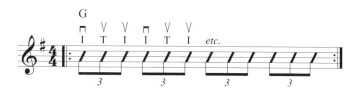

It may feel awkward at first, but with some practice, it will flow into one seamless series of motions. The good thing is that you can perform this at very fast tempos and it always puts the accent on the beat by default.

Thumb-Index-Middle

This is another great pattern with an interesting sound. Start on a downstroke with the thumb. Then continue with an upstroke of the index finger, followed by an upstroke of the middle finger. So, it's:

> 1. Down with the thumb
> 2. Up with the index
> 3. Up with the middle

However, be aware that it's not a standard upstroke with the index finger. In other words, it's not like the second half of a normal down-up strumming pair. That would normally put your middle finger above the strings, as it would follow your index. Instead, you're just going to draw the index finger across the strings, using the first knuckle (the one closest to your hand) in kind of a hooking motion. Then do the same thing with the middle finger.

The great thing about this pattern is the sound. You get this warm, round downstroke with the thumb, followed by two "twinkly"-sounding upstrokes with the fingers:

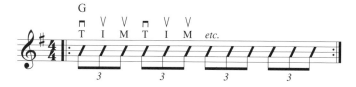

- Using accents can drastically change the effect of a strumming pattern.
- An augmented triad is like a major chord with a raised 5th.
- Roman numerals can be used to identify chords within a key—uppercase for major and lowercase for minor.
- Keep your right hand moving down with every eighth note when strumming 16th-note-based patterns.
- Muted strums are a great way to add depth and texture to strumming patterns.
- There are many different patterns that can be used for strumming triplets, including ones in which more than one strumming finger is used.

SECTION 4

Playing with Style

CHAPTER 13

POP & ROCK

What's Ahead:
- Power chords
- Sus (suspended) chords
- Common pop/rock chord progressions

OK, so now you have a vast array of techniques under your belt. Let's start applying them to some different styles. Although the ukulele has experienced a huge resurgence over the past decade, it still pales in comparison to the guitar or keyboards with regard to airtime. Therefore, while some examples will focus on observable uke techniques found on commercial recordings, a portion of this section will consist of us approximating a guitar or keyboard style on the uke.

This, of course, is the way music has worked over the years. Many phrases that are staples on the guitar, for instance, exist today only because they imitate what was originally performed on a piano or a harmonica, and so on. In other words, what seems eccentric or novel on the uke today may, in fact, become old hat in the near future. It's all music though, and it's always fun when it's played on the uke.

In this chapter, we'll look at the common elements of pop and rock styles and how they apply to the ukulele.

THE POWER CHORD

The power chord played on guitar is what makes the rock world go 'round. But there's absolutely no reason that the uke has to be left out of the fun. A power chord is a two-note chord containing only a root and 5th. Just as with major and minor triads, however, one (or both) of these notes is commonly doubled in a different octave on the guitar. On a uke, due to the reentrant tuning, a note may be doubled in octaves or in unison, depending on its location.

Let's take a look at some power chord forms.

A power chord contains only a root and a 5th. So a C power chord, for example, contains the notes C and G: **C(1)**–D(2)–E(3)–F(4)–**G(5)**. The suffix for a power chord is "5," so a C power chord would be called "C5."

Because power chords don't have a 3rd, they are technically neither major nor minor. They usually sound big, open, powerful, and aggressive instead of happy or sad (there are exceptions to this, of course).

A-Form Power Chord

This form is based off the open A chord. To play it as an open A5, you simply need to mute string 3 by allowing your left-hand middle finger (in this case) to touch it. This is an exception to the "arched finger" rule that we laid out in the early chapters of this book!

A5

In this form, the chord root is on strings 4 and 1. And here's the moveable form as a C5 chord:

The notes on strings 4 and 1 here are the same note, in the same octave, so you could theoretically reduce this form to strings 2 and 1 only, like this:

But doubling the note on string 4 does make a subtle difference, so that's the form we'll use.

C-Form Power Chord

Based off the open C chord, this one will come in two varieties: A three-string version and a four-string version. The chord's root is on string 3.

Here's the three-string version as an open C5:

But in open position, you don't want to worry about avoiding that fourth string, so the four-string version is more practical for strumming:

And here are the moveable forms as D5 chords. Notice the three different fingering suggestions, all of which may work better, depending on the specific situation.

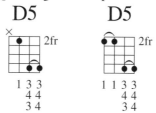

G-Form Power Chord

Finally, we have the G-form power chord, which is based off the open G chord. The root note is on string 2 in this form.

Here's an open G5:

G5

1 2

And here's a B♭5 in moveable form:

B♭5

3fr

1 3 4

Power-Chord Riffs

Let's put these forms to use in some rock-style riffs. Think AC/DC or Led Zeppelin and crank it up! Heck, if you're playing an electric uke (see Chapter 22), kick on a distortion pedal! This first one's in A minor. Aside from the muted 16th-note strums, use all downstrokes for maximum attitude.

audio tracks 138

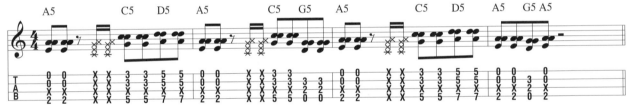

origins

Before the days of distortion pedals and amps with lots of gain (distortion), guitarists had to resort to other methods for generating a crunchy sound. To create the raspy tone for the Kinks' 1964 hit "You Really Got Me," guitarist Dave Davies cut the speaker cone of his Elpico amp with a razor blade. Though he had admittedly done it out of frustration, he was pleasantly surprised by the sound, and it therefore became the key to that song's guitar sound.

We wouldn't recommend cutting your uke with a razor blade, however!

On the next page is a riff in D minor with some 16th-note syncopation. For the C5 on beat 3 of measure 1, place your index finger at fret 3 on strings 2 and 1 for the partial barre, but don't push the strings all the way down. Then lay your middle finger lightly across the strings in front of the index. Strum down for the muted strum, then lift your fret-hand middle finger and push down with your index finger, strumming up for the chord hit. Then release the pressure with your index finger and reapply the mute with your middle finger, strumming down and up for the next two muted strums. Lift the middle finger up and apply pressure again with the index for the chord hit on beat 4. We're kicking on the distortion for this one to prove that ukes *can* rock!

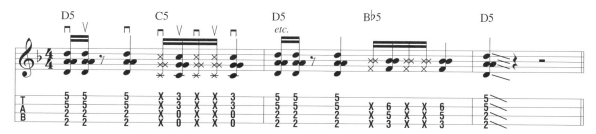

This next riff, in G, uses another guitar-adopted technique called *palm muting*, which results in a muffled, chugging sound. To perform it, lay your right-hand palm on the strings where they touch the bridge. The farther in you move your palm, the more muted the sound will become. Use all downstrokes for this one and try strumming with the thumb. Note that the final chord (on the last eighth note of measure 2), while technically a C5 chord, is not marked as such because it simply functions as a decoration to the G5 chord in this instance.

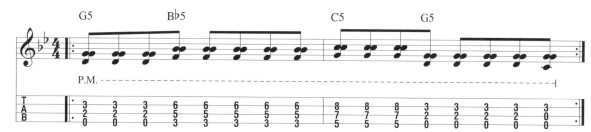

POWER-CHORD SONGS

Let's check out some classic power-chord riffs that we can crank out on the uke. Who needs an amp? Let's open with one of the first power-chord riffs that most guitarists learn. Now you can show them how it's really done! "Rock You Like a Hurricane" is in Em and makes use of both C-form and G-form power-chord shapes. Use all downstrokes and don't neglect the fall-off slide from the E5 chord!

Rock You Like a Hurricane

Words and Music by Rudolf Schenker, Klaus Meine and Herman Rarebell

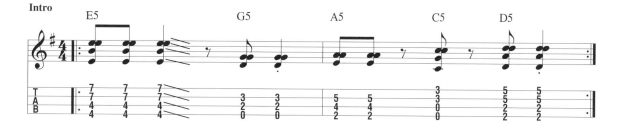

Another classic power-chord riff is the Kinks' "You Really Got Me," also famously covered by Van Halen on their debut album. We'll play this one in D simply because it's the lowest-pitched key on the uke that we can manage for this riff. For the open C5 chord, it's a good idea to use the same fingering for strings 2 and 1 that you're going to use for the D5. That way, you only need to slide back and forth, applying the index-finger barre for the D5 when necessary.

You Really Got Me

Words and Music by Ray Davies

And finally, we come to the king of power-chord riffs: Deep Purple's "Smoke on the Water." This one is all G-form chords.

Smoke on the Water

Words and Music by Ritchie Blackmore, Ian Gillan, Roger Glover, Jon Lord and Ian Paice

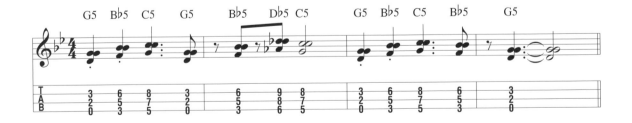

THE SUS (SUSPENDED) CHORD

Another very common chord in pop and rock is the *sus*, or *suspended*, chord. Similar to the power chord, sus chords do not have a 3rd. Instead the 3rd is "suspended"—it's replaced by either the 2nd or the 4th. Doing so creates, respectively, a sus2 (suspended 2nd) or a sus4 (suspended 4th) chord.

Sus4 Chords

The sus4 is more common, so we'll start there. We'll look at each open major chord form and see how it can be converted to a sus4 chord.

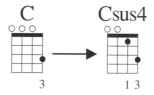

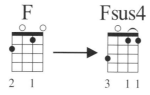

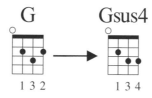

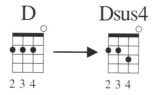

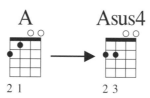

This results in the following moveable sus4 forms. The root of each chord is represented by a hollow circle.

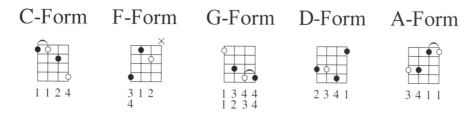

Keep in mind that, although these chords were compared to their major counterparts, suspended chords, like power chords, are neither major nor minor on their own. They're often used as an embellishment to either a major or minor chord, though major chords are certainly more common.

Sus2 Chords

Now let's take a look at some sus2 chords. Again, we'll compare them to their major counterparts. Notice that we need to use a few alternate voicings here to accommodate the suspended 2nd.

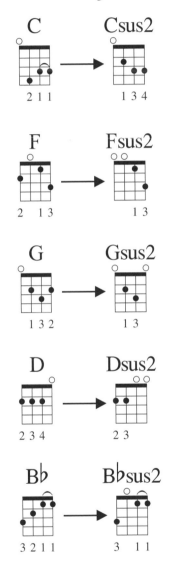

This results in the following moveable sus2 forms. Again, the roots are indicated with a hollow circle.

Do you notice anything familiar about these shapes? If they look a lot like the sus4 forms, you're right! It's a peculiar fact that sus chords pull double duty. A sus4 chord can always be seen as a sus2 chord from a different root, and vice versa. So, the F-form sus2 could also be a C-form sus4, etc. Musical context will usually dictate the proper name.

SUS-CHORD SONGS

Let's check out these sus chords in some classic song riffs. Let's start with one of the most famous sus-chord riffs of all: Tom Petty's "Free Fallin'." We'll play it here in the original key of F.

Free Fallin'

Words and Music by Tom Petty and Jeff Lynne

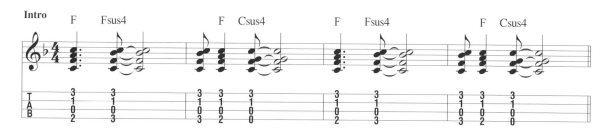

The Who's Pete Townshend is one the biggest proponents of the sus chord, and it's prominently displayed in "Pinball Wizard." Here it is in the original key of B. This is great practice for your 16th-note strumming too. Watch the accent marks!

Pinball Wizard

Words and Music by Peter Townshend

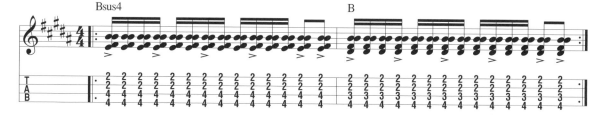

COMMON ROCK AND POP PROGRESSIONS

Let's finish this chapter by taking a look at some chord progressions that have stood the test of time in rock and pop styles.

I–V–vi–IV

The first is a I–V–vi–IV. This progression—and variants that begin at other points in the progression (such as vi–IV–I–V, etc.)—has graced literally thousands of songs, including U2's "With or Without You" and the Beatles' "Let It Be," to name only two.

Search "Axis of Awesome 4 chords" on YouTube to hear just a sampling of the countless songs that use this progression, blended into one extended medley.

A I–V–vi–IV in the key of G, for example, would be G–D–Em–C.

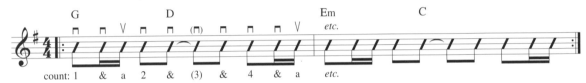

♭VI–♭VII–i

This is a minor-key progression that climbs from the sixth chord to the seventh chord, and finally, to the tonic minor chord. It, along with the backwards version (i–♭VII–♭VI), has fueled the engine of countless hard rock songs, including Danzig's "Mother" and Led Zeppelin's "Stairway to Heaven."

In the key of A minor, this would be F–G–Am.

I–♭VII–IV

This is a classic rock staple. In the key of D, it would be D–C–G.

I–IV

Just loop these two chords forever. If done well, you can squeeze dozens of songs out of them. Just ask U2! In A major, this would be A and D.

- A power chord contains a root and 5th. It's neither major nor minor.

- A sus4 chord contains a root, 4th, and 5th.

- A sus2 chord contains a root, 2nd, and 5th.

- Sus chords are neither major nor minor by themselves, but they're often used to decorate a major or minor chord.

- Many songs use the same chord progressions, only in different keys and with different rhythmic feels.

CHAPTER 14
JAZZ & BLUES

What's Ahead:

- 6 and 6/9 chords
- Extended (ninth, 11th, and 13th) chords
- Common jazz and blues progressions
- Blues turnaround licks
- Blues scale
- Bending strings
- Mixolydian mode
- Jazz and blues licks

Now we turn attention to the world of blues and jazz, which are truly fun styles to play on the uke. Check out the awesome legacy of Lyle Ritz in this regard and more recently the arrangements by James Hill and Jake Shimabukuro to hear what can be done in this vein.

JAZZ AND BLUES CHORDS BOOT CAMP

The chords used in jazz and blues are usually a bit more sophisticated than those in pop and rock; you generally don't find too many triads. Instead, you find more colorful harmonies like 6 chords, 6/9 chords, seventh chords, and extended chords such as ninths, 11ths, and 13ths. So let's get some of these sounds under our fingers to expand our vocabulary once again!

6 Chords

A 6 chord is basically a major triad with an added 6th tone, so it contains a root, 3rd, 5th, and 6th. C6 is spelled C–E–G–A, and it's very easy to play on the uke.

C6

Does that chord look familiar? If so, there's good reason. We learned it earlier as Am7. So, what gives? Well, nothing gives. They're the same chord. It's kind of like the relative major and minor thing: They both contain the same four notes, but if you consider C the root, it's a C6 chord, and if you consider A the root, it's an Am7 chord.

For our purposes here, we're going to stick to moveable forms because jazz songs tend to wander through various keys, so chances are, you're going to be playing a lot of moveable chords anyway.

Major 6 Chords—6

Here are several voicings for a major 6 chord. The root is a hollow circle in each form.

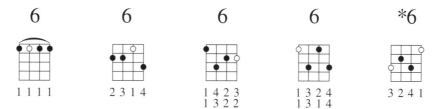

*This voicing only contains the root, 3rd, and 6th (no 5th), but it's still a usable 6-chord form.

Minor 6 Chords—m6

A minor 6 chord contains a root, ♭3rd, 5th, and 6th. The only difference between it and a major 6 chord is the ♭3rd. Cm6 is spelled C–E♭–G–A. Here are several m6 forms:

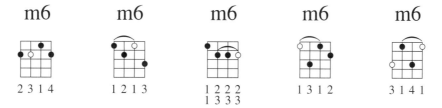

Compare each m6 voicing to the matching major 6 voicing above to see how they're altered. In each one, you'll find that only one note (the 3rd) has been altered.

6/9 Chords

A 6/9 chord adds both a 6th and a 9th to a triad. What's a 9th? Well, it's the same as the 2nd, only an octave higher. C6/9 is spelled C–E–G–A–D. But wait—we only have four strings on the uke! What do we do? Well, we omit a note. Obviously, it can't be a 6/9 chord if it doesn't have a 6th and a 9th in it, so we have to keep them. And it can't be a major 6/9 if it doesn't have a 3rd, so we should keep that note also. That means we either need to omit the 5th or the root. Granted, it seems odd to omit the root, but remember that, if you're playing with someone else, they'll most likely be playing the root of the chord. And even if they're not, it's usually implied by the musical context.

Major 6/9 Chords—6/9

Here are some major 6/9 voicings—again, with a hollow circle indicating the root. When the root is not present, it will be shown as a black diamond.

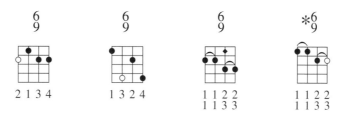

*This voicing only contains the root, 5th, 6th, and 9th (no 3rd). So, it can technically be used as a major *or* minor 6/9 chord.

Minor 6/9 Chords—m6/9

A minor 6/9 contains the root, ♭3rd, 5th, 6th, and 9th. Cm6/9 is spelled C–E♭–G–A–D. Here are some moveable m6/9 forms:

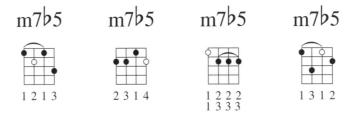

m$_9^6$	m$_9^6$	m$_9^6$	*m$_9^6$
2 1 3 4	1 3 2 4	1 2 3 4 1 2 3 3	1 1 2 2 1 1 3 3

*This voicing only contains the root, 5th, 6th, and 9th (no 3rd). So, it can technically be used as a major *or* minor 6/9 chord.

Suspended Seventh Chords

We looked at sus chords last chapter. Now we'll look at the seventh versions of those chords.

Seventh sus4 Chords—7sus4

A 7sus4 chord contains a root, 4th, 5th, and ♭7th. C7sus4 is spelled C–F–G–B♭. Because it has no 3rd, it is technically neither dominant nor minor. However, it often functions as a substitute for a dominant seventh chord. Here are some moveable forms. Compare these to the dominant seventh forms you learned in Chapter 9.

7sus4	7sus4	7sus4	7sus4
1 3 1 1	2 3 1 4	1 3 2 4	1 1 2 2 1 1 3 3

Minor Seventh Flat-Five Chords

A minor seventh flat-five chord is just what it sounds like: a minor seventh chord with a ♭5th degree. Cm7♭5 is spelled C–E♭–G♭–B♭.

Minor Seventh Flat-Five Chords—m7♭5

m7♭5	m7♭5	m7♭5	m7♭5
1 2 1 3	2 3 1 4	1 2 2 2 1 3 3 3	1 3 1 2

Note that these chords are also known as minor 6 chords with a different root. Compare the shapes to the minor 6 chords to see what we mean. The shapes are the same, but the root notes are different.

Diminished Seventh Chords

A diminished seventh chord contains a root, 3rd, ♭5th, and ♭♭7th (6th). The ♭♭7th note is *enharmonic* to the 6th, which means that the two notes sound the same even though they have different names. For example, B♯ and C are enharmonic (there's no note between B and C, so if you try to raise B a half step by adding a sharp to it, it'll sound just like C). This chord is symmetrical—all four notes in the chord are equally spaced. This means that any of the four notes can act as the root.

Diminished Seventh Chords—°7

C°7 is spelled C–E♭–G♭–A. You can move this chord form up or down four frets at a time, and you'll still be playing the same notes. This is why only one form is shown, with no root indicated: Any note in this form can act as the root.

°7

1 3 2 4

Ninth Chords

Ninth chords are a type of *extended chord*. This means that we continue stacking notes past the octave. A seventh chord contains a root, 3rd, 5th, and 7th; a ninth chord continues that stacking procedure by adding a 9th on top.

Major Ninth Chords—maj9

A major ninth chord contains a root, 3rd, 5th, 7th, and 9th. Cmaj9 is spelled C–E–G–B–D. Again, we have to omit one of the notes to make this chord playable on the uke.

maj9   maj9   maj9

2 1 4 3   2 3 1 4   1 4 2 3
                           1 3 2 2

Minor Ninth Chords—m9

A minor ninth chord contains a root, ♭3rd, 5th, ♭7th, and 9th. Cm9 is spelled C–E♭–G–B♭–D.

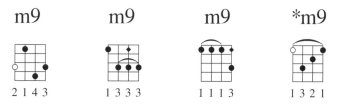

m9   m9   m9   *m9

2 1 4 3   1 3 3 3   1 1 1 3   1 3 2 1

*This voicing only contains the root, 5th, ♭7th, and 9th (no 3rd). So, it can technically be used as a dominant or minor ninth chord.

Dominant Ninth Chords—9

A dominant ninth chord contains a root, 3rd, 5th, ♭7th, and 9th. C9 is spelled C–E–G–B♭–D.

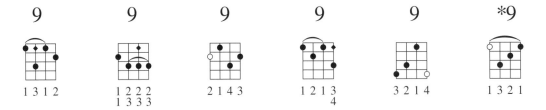

*This voicing only contains the root, 5th, ♭7th, and 9th (no 3rd). So, it can technically be used as a dominant or minor ninth chord.

Ninth Sus4 Chords—9sus4

A 9sus4 chord contains a root, 4th, 5th, ♭7th, and 9th. C9sus4 is spelled C–F–G–B♭–D. Because it has no 3rd, it is technically neither dominant nor minor. However, it often functions as a substitute for a dominant seventh chord.

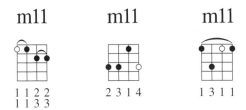

11th Chords

An 11th chord continues the stacking procedure by adding an 11th on top, so it technically contains a root, 3rd, 5th, 7th, 9th, and 11th. However, in practice, the 11th clashes with the 3rd, so you don't usually see pure major 11th or dominant 11th chords.

Minor 11th Chords—m11

A m11 chord contains a root, ♭3rd, 5th, ♭7th, 9th, and 11th. A Cm11 chord is spelled C–E♭–G–B♭–D–F. Obviously we have to drop two notes to play them on a uke. This is usually either the root, 5th, or 9th.

13th Chords

Finally, we come to the last stop, 13th chords. These chords contain a root, 3rd, 5th, 7th, 9th, 11th, and 13th. Again, the 11th is not usually included in major or dominant 13th chords. The most essential tones are the root, 3rd, 7th, and 13th, although the root may be omitted sometimes as well.

Major 13th Chords—maj13

A major 13th contains a root, 3rd, 5th, 7th, 9th, and 13th. Cmaj13 is spelled C–E–G–B–D–A.

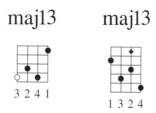

Minor 13th Chords—m13

A minor 13th chord contains a root, ♭3rd, 5th, ♭7th, 9th, 11th, and 13th. Cm13 is spelled C–E♭–G–B♭–D–F–A.

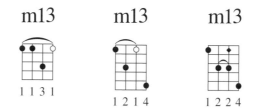

Dominant 13th Chords—13

A dominant 13th chord contains a root, 3rd, 5th, ♭7th, 9th, and 13th. C13 is spelled C–E–G–B♭–D–A.

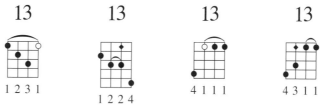

13th Sus4 Chords—13sus4

A 13sus4 chord contains a root, 4th, 5th, ♭7th, 9th, and 13th. C13sus4 is spelled C–F–G–B♭–D–A. Because it has no 3rd, it is technically neither dominant nor minor. However, it often functions as a substitute for a dominant seventh chord.

nuts
& bolts

Extended chords—ninths, 11ths, and 13ths—basically act as a substitute for seventh chords. They're a little fancier-sounding and have a more specific sound. So any time you see a dominant 13th chord, for example, you could play a dominant seventh instead. It won't sound as fancy, but it won't contain any wrong notes. Or, if you see a major ninth chord, you could play a major seventh instead. Again, it won't contain any wrong notes.

BLUES AND JAZZ CHORD PROGRESSIONS

Now let's put some of these chords to use with common progressions in the blues and jazz styles. Although the two are often intermingled, we'll break them up into two categories.

Common Blues Progressions

The most common blues progression of all is called the *12-bar blues*. In its simplest form, it consists of the I, IV, and V chords of a key. The chords are most often played as some type of dominant chord, such as a seventh or ninth. The jazzier blues styles will make use of 13th chords as well.

In the key of C, a 12-bar blues will contain C (I), F (IV), and G (V) dominant chords. Let's check out the basic form, which will use dominant seventh chords throughout. We'll play it with a shuffle feel, using a syncopated rhythm.

And here's a funky blues in D that makes use of moveable ninth chords: D9, G9, and A9. In addition to some 16th-note syncopation and muted strums, we're sliding into each chord from a half step below—a funk staple.

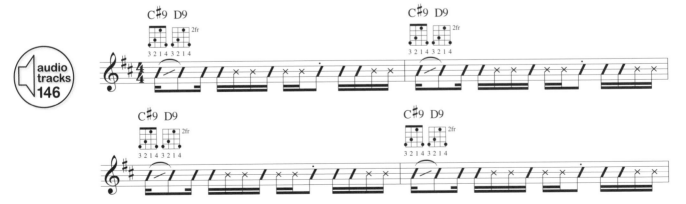

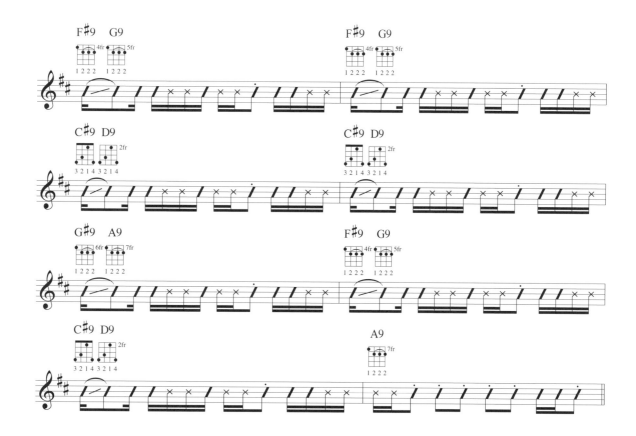

Another common blues progression is the 8-bar blues, which you can hear in songs like "Key to the Highway" and "It Hurts Me Too." The form isn't as standardized as the 12-bar blues (in fact, the two previously named songs use different progressions), but here's a very common form. We'll play it in A, using a fingerpicking pattern. The final two measures contain what's called a *turnaround phrase*. We'll look more at those in a bit.

Common Jazz Progressions

There are several jazz progressions that are common as well, but let's first head back to 12-bar land. Indeed, the 12-bar blues progression is a staple of jazz as well, but jazzers tend to dress it up a bit with more chords and more sophistication.

Let's play through a jazz blues in C with a shuffle feel (usually called a "swing" feel in jazz). We'll play mostly quarter notes, but we'll also throw in a few slides and some syncopated chords for a more authentic feel.

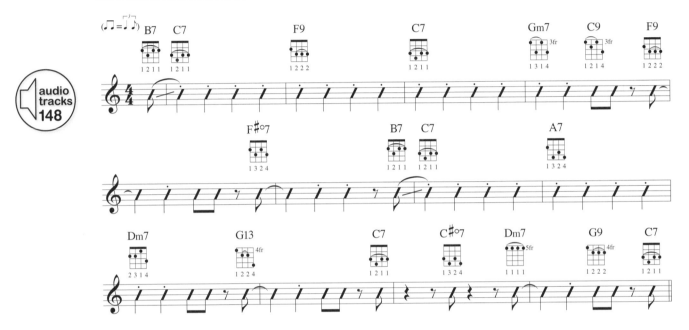

Another staple of jazz is the ii–V–I progression. In the key of C major, this would be Dm7–G7–C (or C6, Cmaj7, etc.). Many jazz tunes feature ii–V–I progressions in many different keys. Here's an example of that idea. We'll see ii–V–I progressions first in C major, then in B♭ major, and finally in E♭ major. By doing this, we'll make use of many forms of each chord.

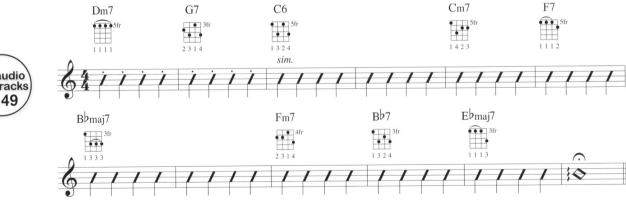

A variation of the ii–V–I progression is the I–VI–ii–V, which, when looped, has a ii–V–I within it: I–VI–**ii–V, I**–VI–ii–V, etc. This is known as a jazz turnaround, and in C it would be C–A7–Dm7–G7. If you noticed, this progression appeared in our jazz 12-bar blues.

Another common move in many jazz tunes is the *cycle of 4ths* progression. This is a chain of chords that move up a 4th incrementally. In other words, an A chord would be followed by a D chord (**A**–B–C–**D**), a D chord would be followed by a G chord (**D**–E–F–**G**), and a G chord would be followed by a C chord (**G**–A–B–**C**), etc.

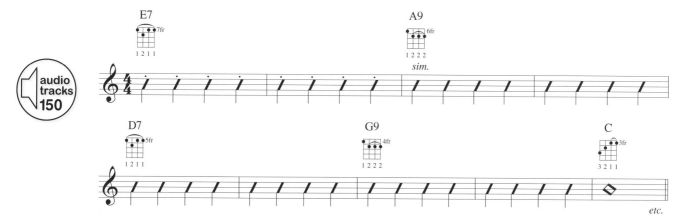

This cycle-of-4ths move is the standard bridge (B section) in "rhythm changes," a 32-bar song form based off Gershwin's "I Got Rhythm." The rest of the song is largely built upon a repeating I–VI–ii–V pattern.

BLUES TURNAROUND LICKS

As we saw earlier, the most common progression in blues is the 12-bar. Most of the time, a turn-around appears in measures 11–12. This is a phrase that begins at the I chord and, usually via chromatic movement, leads to the V chord in measure 12, which "turns around" the progression to start a new "chorus" (another 12 bars) of blues.

Here, we'll take a look at different turnaround licks in several different keys so you can turn some heads the next time you're at an open-mic jam. All of these turnarounds will start at bar 11 of the 12-bar form, so they'll just be two measures long.

Our first turnaround is in the key of C. After strumming the C7 chord on the downbeat, fret the descending two-note *double stops* (two notes played simultaneously) on strings 3 and 2 with the ring and middle fingers, respectively. This will allow you to lay your index finger lightly across the strings behind them to keep everything quiet. In other words, you can strum away without having to worry about avoiding strings 4 and 1.

Next up is a turnaround in the key of A, in a fingerpicking style. Notice the grace-note hammer-on at the beginning of measure 2; this is a classic blues move on guitar and piano.

Here's another one in C, this time exploiting the reentrant tuning for a nice effect.

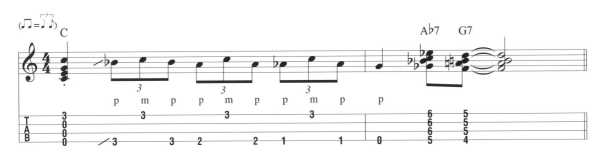

And finally, here's one in G that sounds great strummed with the thumb. Notice the staccato marks; they make all the difference.

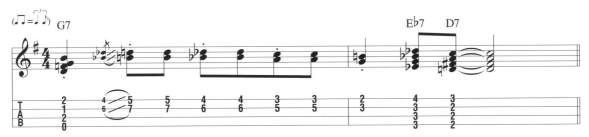

There are several common elements in a turnaround lick:
- Begin with the I chord (or the tonic note of the key) on beat 1 of measure 11.
- Beat 2 normally begins the chromatic portion of the lick that lasts three beats.
- The I chord re-emerges on beat 1 of measure 12.
- This is followed by the V chord, which is usually approached from a half step above.

THE BLUES SCALE

Now that we've got a slew of jazz and blues chords under our fingers, let's turn our attention to some lead uke in these styles. First item on the agenda is a new scale called, fittingly, the *blues scale*. Remember those minor pentatonic scale forms you learned in Chapter 10? Well, dust those off again because the blues scale is very similar. In fact, it's the same scale as minor pentatonic but with one added note: The ♭5th.

Whereas the minor pentatonic contains the tonic, ♭3rd, 4th, 5th, and ♭7th, the blues scale adds the ♭5th to the proceedings. So the A blues scale is spelled A–C–D–E♭–E–G. (Note that the ♭5th may also be written as its harmonic equivalent, the ♯4th, in the music, depending on the musical context.)

Open Blues Scale Forms

Here's what the A blues scale, which has the tonic on string 1, looks like in open position:

And here's the open D blues scale, which has the tonic on string 3:

Moveable Blues Scale Form 1

Now let's take the moveable minor pentatonic form 1 that we learned in Chapter 10 and turn it into a blues scale. Again, this is based off the open A blues scale, which has the tonic on string 1. That'll look like this:

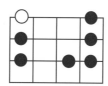

Extended Blues Scale Form 1

And here's the extended form, to which we'll add an extra ♭5th note on top.

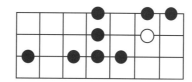

Moveable Blues Scale Form 2

Based off the open D blues scale, with the tonic on string 3, moveable form 2 looks like this:

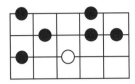

Extended Blues Scale Form 2

And here's the extended form 2, which has a tonic on string 3 and one an octave higher on string 1.

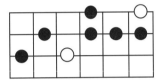

BLUES SCALE LICKS

Now let's check out how we can make this scale talk. We'll make use of each scale form and identify which is being used for each lick.

This first one comes from the open D blues scale. Blues phrasing is all about the subtleties, so it's crucial to pay extra attention to all the slides, grace notes, staccato markings, etc.

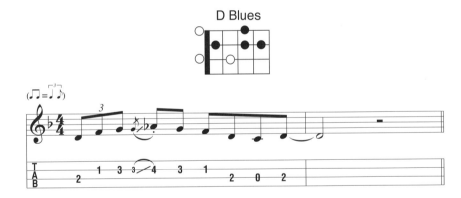

Here's one from the extended B blues scale form 1. Notice the slides up from and down to the blues note (♭5th)—a very common maneuver.

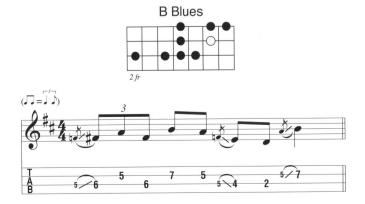

Bending Strings

If you've ever watched a blues guitarist, you've no doubt witnessed string bending in action. When you bend a string (i.e., push or pull it up or down), you increase the tension on the string and, in turn, raise the pitch. The more you bend, the more the pitch raises.

The amount of pitch bend can range from a quarter step (which is "in the cracks," or halfway to a half step), to a half step (distance of one fret), a whole step (distance of two frets), or more. For now, we're going to stick to the quarter-step and half-step varieties.

These are very expressive techniques that can really make your blues phrases come alive. The idea is to simply push the string up toward the ceiling while holding it.

Quarter-Step Bend

A quarter-step bend is "in the cracks." In other words, you're playing a note that can't be played by conventional fretting because it doesn't exist. It's sharper than the current fret but flatter than the next.

To get this idea down, we'll work out of our C blues scale form 1 shape in third position:

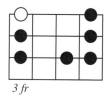

3 fr

In this shape, the quarter-step bend sounds best on the sixth-fret notes on strings 2 and 1. So let's try the following simple exercise. You don't have to bend too far; you don't want the pitch to match fret 7. At first, compare your bent sixth-fret note to a normal seventh-fret note to make sure you're not bending that far.

> It's a good idea to support your bending finger with another finger behind it if possible. If you're bending with your ring finger, for instance, use your middle finger behind it for support. It's not terribly necessary when bending only a quarter step, but it's a good habit to start early because, if you ever want to bend much farther, such as a whole step, you'll definitely want to support that bending finger!

In the music, a quarter-step bend is shown as a short upward-curving line. In the tab, bends are always shown with an arrow from the number and a fraction or number denoting the distance of the bend.

Half-Step Bend

The half-step bend is the actual distance of one fret in pitch, so it requires a bit more of a bend. Staying in our same C blues scale form as the last example, the best spot for this bend is on fret 5 of string 3. This will bend the 4th of the scale up to the ♭5th (the "blue note").

Half-step bends are notated differently in the notation: A stemless grace note shows the starting pitch, which is connected to the target pitch via a V-shape symbol (pointing up or down, depending on the range of the note).

Of course, you don't have to bend as a grace note; you can bend in rhythm as well. In this example, we're bending and then releasing the bend in time.

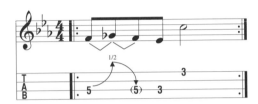

We already looked at blues scale form 1. Now let's take a quick look at the other blues-scale forms to see where these bends can be used.

Blues Scale Form 2

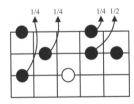

Extended Blues Scale Form 1

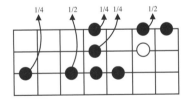

Extended Blues Scale Form 2

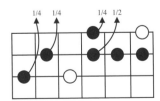

String-Bending Licks

OK, let's get back to the licks. It's time to put our new bends to use. Here's one in E:

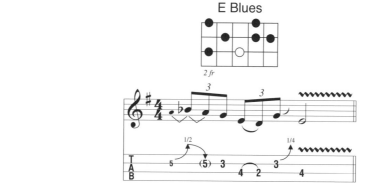

That horizontal, wavy line over the last note in the previous example is a *vibrato* marking. Vibrato is a steady fluctuation in pitch that imitates the same effect used by vocalists. It's a very expressive device that can add some vocal-like qualities to your phrases.

Vibrato is achieved by slightly bending the string and releasing it over and over again at a steady rate. It's easier to achieve toward the middle of the length of a string rather than near the nut. Developing a good vibrato takes some practice, but it's a wonderful technique to acquire, and definitely worth the trouble.

Here's a nice lick in C that makes use of some staccato in a B.B. King fashion. Keep those notes short!

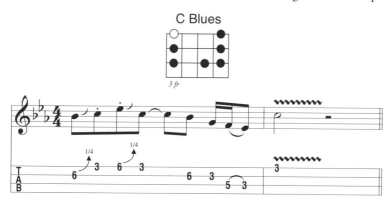

Finally, here's one from the open form of the A extended blues scale. Be sure to let the notes ring together for the first three beats.

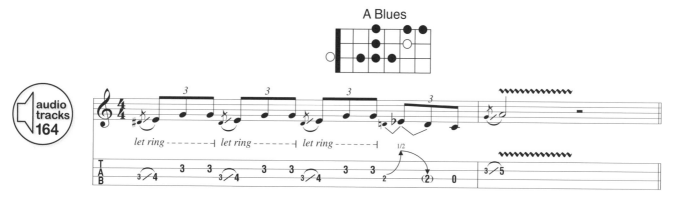

Just because it's called the "blues scale" doesn't mean you can only use it in blues songs. Many of the licks we've looked at thus far would sound perfectly at home in jazz, rock, pop, or country songs. The blues scale, much like the pentatonic scales, is prevalent in nearly all styles of music.

THE MIXOLYDIAN MODE

Let's learn one more scale for good measure. The Mixolydian mode is just like a major scale except it has a ♭7th note. Let's use our open C major scale as an example.

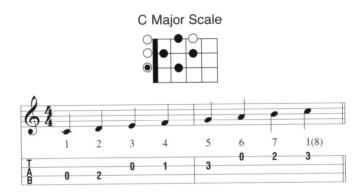

In order to make this the C Mixolydian mode, we need to lower the 7th note, B, by a half step to B♭.

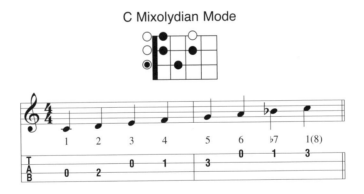

If this scale form looks familiar to you, it's not because you're going crazy. In fact, we did learn this exact scale form in Chapter 7, where we called it the F major scale. So, what gives? Well, both are correct. C Mixolydian and F major share the exact same notes. It's similar to the relative-minor concept. If you consider C the tonic, it's the C Mixolydian mode; if you consider F the tonic, it's the F major scale.

In fact, there are modes for each note of the major scale. In other words, you can consider any note of the major scale the tonic, and that will result in the name of another mode. So since there are seven notes in a major scale, there are seven modes in all.

Moveable Major and Mixolydian Forms

Although we learned moveable forms for the major pentatonic scale, we never did learn them for the major scale, so let's digress just a second and learn our two major scale forms as moveable forms.

Moveable Major Scale Form 1

This form is based on the open C major scale and has the tonic on strings 3 and 1.

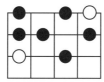

Moveable Major Scale Form 2

This form is based on the open F major scale and has the tonic on string 2. It spans from the 5th to the 5th.

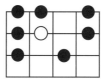

Moveable Mixolydian Mode Form 1

This will be just like the major form, only with a lowered 7th. Again, the tonic will be on strings 3 and 1.

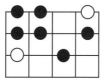

Moveable Mixolydian Mode Form 2

This form has the tonic on string 2 and spans from the 5th to the 5th.

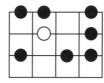

MIXOLYDIAN MODE LICKS

Now let's learn a few jazzy-sounding licks from the Mixolydian mode. Again, we'll indicate which scale form is being used for each lick. First up is a lick from A Mixolydian.

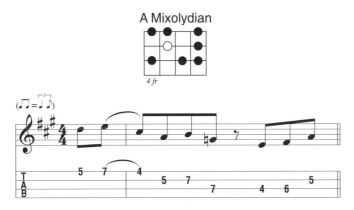

And here's a nice one from D Mixolydian. For the final pull-off on string 2, you'll need to pre-position your index finger on its pad so that it can roll over to string 3 for the final D note.

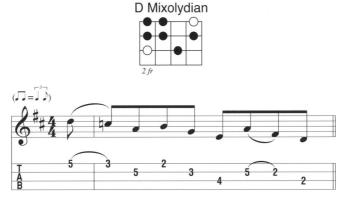

Chromatic Passing Tones

A very common device in jazz playing is the *chromatic passing tone*. This is the concept of connecting two scale tones with a chromatic note that lies between them.

For example, if you look at our two Mixolydian scale forms below, you can see that all of these "in-between" notes are indicated by gray dots.

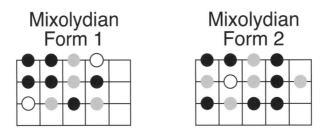

Any and all of these in-between notes are fair game with regard to dressing up your phrases. However, while there are no rules in music, there are some guidelines that will help you produce phrases that are considered by most to be "musical." It mainly comes down to two things:

1. Don't end a phrase on one of these notes. They don't make for a pleasing resolution and, instead, are best used in passing (hence the name).
2. Try to place these passing tones on the weak beats. So if you're playing a phrase in eighth notes, try to place the passing tones on the "and" of the beat. If you're playing 16th notes, try to place the passing tones on the "e" or the "a" of the beat.

Again, these aren't hard-and-fast rules, but they'll treat you right most of the time. Let's hear some of these passing tones in action. Each passing tone will be identified in the music so you can see how they're operating.

Here's a line from G Mixolydian that uses a passing tone between the 5th and 4th of the scale:

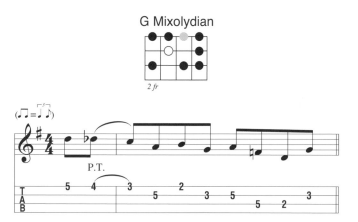

This phrase in B♭ makes use of two passing tones: One ascending and one descending. The fingering can be a bit tricky, so check out the suggestions.

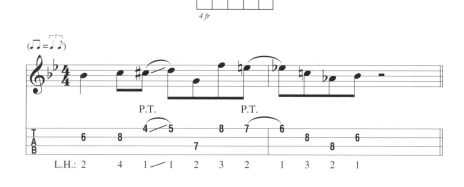

Finally, we have a line in E that demonstrates another important concept: These chromatic tones don't always have to be used as passing tones; they can also be used as *approach tones*—tones that approach a scale tone from a half step below or above. We see three chromatic tones in this line, each used in a different way:

- The first is a passing tone connecting E to D.
- The second is an approach tone that resolves to F♯ from a half step above (G♮).
- The third is a grace-note approach note that resolves to G♯ from a half step below (G♮).

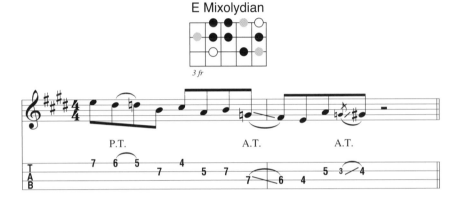

- 6 and 6/9 chords are a substitute for major and minor triads.
- Extended chords (ninths, 11ths, and 13ths) are a substitute for seventh chords.
- The 12-bar blues is the most common blues form and uses I, IV, and V chords, normally played as dominant sevenths or ninths.
- The 8-bar blues is another common blues form.
- A 12-bar jazz blues uses more chords than a typical standard blues.
- Measures 11–12 of a 12-bar blues contain the turnaround—a phrase that travels from the I chord to the V, usually by way of chromatic movement.
- A jazz turnaround progression uses a I–VI–ii–V progression.
- The ii–V–I is perhaps the most common jazz progression of all, and many tunes contain this progression in several different keys.
- The cycle of 4ths progression (E7–A7–D7–G7, etc.) is common in jazz and is famously used as the bridge in "rhythm changes" (Gershwin's "I Got Rhythm").
- The blues scale is a minor pentatonic scale with an added ♭5th.
- String bending and vibrato can be used to imbue your phrases with a very vocal quality.
- The Mixolydian mode is like a major scale but with a ♭7th tone.
- Chromatic passing tones are commonly used in jazz phrases to connect two scale tones. They're usually placed on weak parts of the beat.
- Chromatic tones are also commonly used in jazz as approach tones—notes that resolve up or down by a half step to a target note.

Full Song Transcriptions

CHAPTER 15
"RIPTIDE"

What's Ahead:

- Varying strum patterns
- Pentatonic riffs
- Muted Strums
- 16th-note syncopations
- Routing directions

A big indie hit in 2013 for then-newcomer Vance Joy, "Riptide" is driven throughout by his strummed ukulele. However, it's a bit of an anomaly, as it features a tuning setup that we haven't discussed yet. Vance played a tenor ukulele on the song, but it was strung up and tuned like a baritone, only in reentrant tuning! So it's tuned D–G–B–E, but the D is an octave up.

This tuning was confirmed by Vance on his Facebook page. But there's one more problem. The original recording sounds a half step higher than the chord shapes he can be seen playing in live appearances. In other words, the recording sounds in the key of C♯ (or D♭), but when he plays the song live, it sounds in C. This means that he must have either used a capo on fret 1 in the studio, or the pitch of the recording was altered.

Regardless, we'll arrange it here for standard reentrant ukulele tuning, and we'll play it in the key of C. In order to play along with the original recording, you can place a uke capo on fret 1. A *capo* is a device that clamps onto your strings, essentially "barring" them for you.

THE CHORDS AND RHYTHM

The majority of "Riptide" makes use of a three-chord progression in C major, Am–G–C, in which Am and G last for two beats and C lasts for one measure. The intro and verses of the song mostly employ this strum pattern:

count: 1 & (2) e & a 3 & (4) e & a

For the choruses, the progression stays the same, but Vance alters the strum pattern to include muted strums. These muted strums are created a bit differently than the ones we looked at in Chapter 12, though. The effect is created entirely with the strumming hand. Strum down and plant your right-hand palm on the strings as you strum. The resultant "thwack" sound is a combination of your strumming finger and your palm hitting the strings/neck simultaneously. After performing this move, your strumming finger should be in position to immediately follow with an upstroke.

Note that, on the recording, Vance doubled the uke part throughout, which accounts for the thick sound.

INTERLUDE RIFF

After the second chorus, there's a brief instrumental interlude in which Vance plays a syncopated C major pentatonic melody. Because he's playing in baritone tuning, he fingers this riff differently than we're able to (and of course, all the chord shapes are different as well), but we can get the notes right, and the effect sounds very close to the original.

The riff is working out of the extended C major pentatonic form 1 that we learned in Chapter 10. However, we're also making use of the open second string in order to better approximate the sound on the recording.

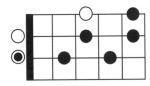

THE BRIDGE

The bridge makes use of a new chord progression, adding an F chord to the mix. He also alters the rhythmic feel here, still strumming 16th notes but with a new syncopation. Remember to keep your strumming hand moving constantly and accent with harder strums when necessary. Here's what the strum pattern looks like:

ROUTING DIRECTIONS

After the chorus following the bridge, we see a *routing direction*. The "D.S. al Coda" here stands for the Italian phrase "Dal segno to the tail." It instructs you to go back to the D.S. sign, which looks like a fancy "S" with a line through it, with dots on both sides (𝄋), and then play until you reach the "To Coda" direction. At that point, you skip to the Coda section, signified by the big target-looking symbol.

Riptide

Words and Music by Vance Joy

31 C / Fmaj7

I can't have it, I can't have it an-y oth-er way I

33 Am / G / C

swear she's des-tined for the screen.

35 Am / G / C

Clos-est thing to Mi-chelle Pfeif-fer that you've ev-er seen, oh.

Chorus
Uke: w/ Rhy. Fig. 2 (3 times)
37 Am / G / C

La-dy, run-nin' down to the rip-tide, tak-en a-way to the

39 Am / G / C

dark side. I wan-na be your left hand man. I

CHAPTER 16
"I'LL SEE YOU IN MY DREAMS"

What's Ahead:

- Alternate chord voicings
- Triplet strum flourishes
- Dissonant chord forms

Joe Brown was a close friend of fellow uke enthusiast George Harrison, and he joined the many talented performers paying tribute to the man for the Concert for George benefit show at the Royal Albert Hall on November 29, 2002. Among other songs, he performed a touching rendition of the 1924 standard "I'll See You in My Dreams" as the finale. The song has been covered many times throughout the years by various performers, including Chet Atkins/Mark Knopfler, Eddie Cochran, Ingrid Michaelson, and Alden Howard, to name a few.

The song is performed in standard uke tuning in the key of F major. Brown strums through much of the song, mostly using open-position chords, but he adds a good bit of fingerpicking for variety as well. Note that we've also arranged a second guitar part for ukulele, so watch for that to pop in and out a few times.

INTRO AND VERSE

Brown opens the song with a strum riff that moves as follows: F–F6–Fmaj7–F6. The strumming here is essentially a two-measure pattern with an eighth-note syncopation appearing in the second bar. Notice also the alternate voicing for Fmaj7:

Fmaj7

Technically, this is an A5 chord as it only contains A and E notes, but it functions here as Fmaj7 because of the context.

The verse initially begins with the same two-measure strum pattern, but it quickly begins to veer toward less syncopation and more quarter-note emphasis as more chords are introduced.

PRE-CHORUS

For the pre-chorus, Joe thins out the texture, moving to three-note voicings on strings 3–1 as the dynamic drops a bit. We also see him begin to incorporate triplet flourishes into his strumming pattern. For these triplets, Joe uses a pattern of down (index)–down (thumb)–up (index).

You can see him demonstrate this pattern clearly, which he calls a "scissor movement," by searching "Joe Brown ukulele lesson" on YouTube.

INTERLUDE

For the interlude, Joe begins to employ fingerpicking in all kinds of interesting ways, creating rolling arpeggio patterns and melodic accents. Check out the beautifully dissonant voicing over the C7 chord in measures 71 and 72, in which he rubs an E♭ (or D♯) note on string 3 against the open E string to create a C7♯9 chord:

C7♯9

I'll See You in My Dreams

Words by Gus Kahn
Music by Isham Jones

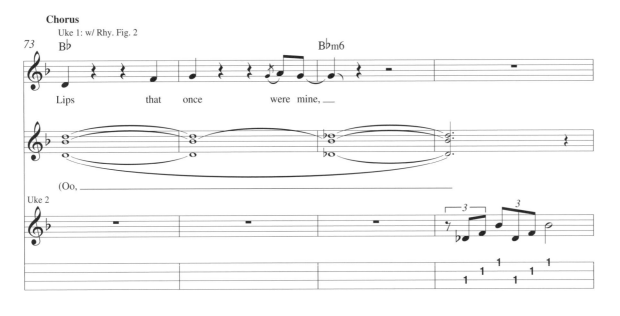

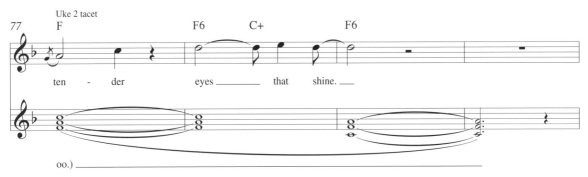

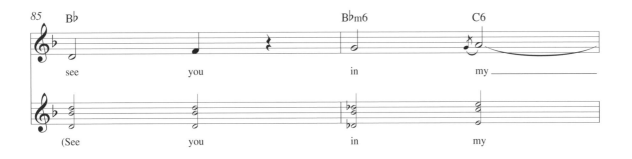

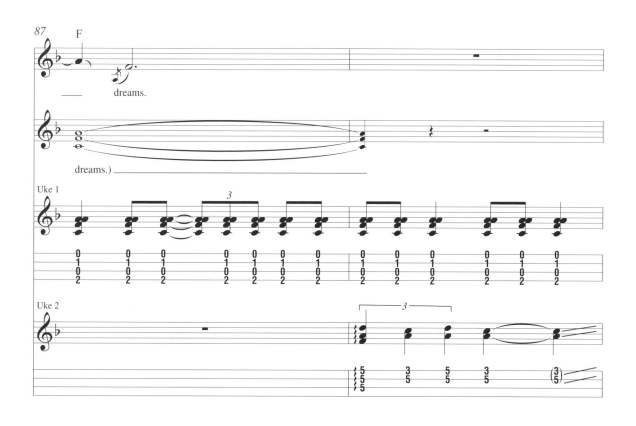

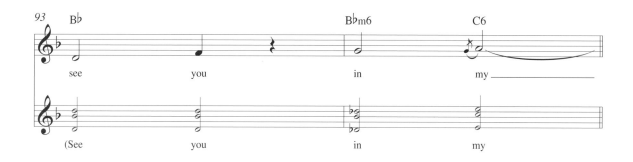

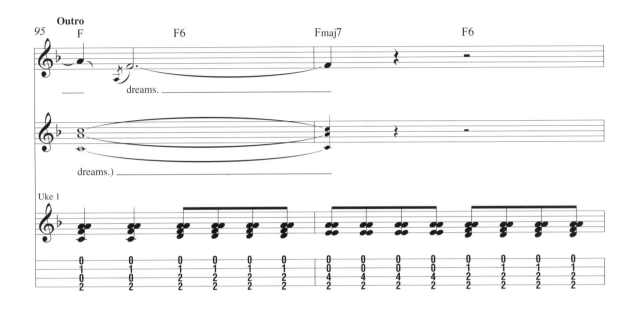

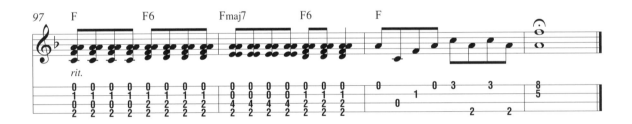

CHAPTER 17
"5 YEARS TIME"

What's Ahead:

- Muted strums
- New fingerpicking patterns
- Major pentatonic melodies

The English band Noah and the Whale had a hit in 2008 with the fun, quirky "5 Years Time," complete with a hilarious Wes Anderson-esque video featuring matching blue-and-yellow Boy Scout-type outfits with calf-high socks. (Be sure to check it out if you haven't seen it yet!) The song is driven by a ukulele—two, in fact!—and it only makes sense; what other instrument could support the song's happy-go-lucky message with such authority?

CHORDS AND RHYTHM

"5 Years Time" is about as simple as it gets with regard to chords. There are only three of them: C, F, and G. It's those I, IV, and V chords again! However, the band does a nice job of keeping the song interesting by varying the textures and melodies throughout.

Strum Pattern

Along with the open C, F, and G chords, you can play 90 percent of the song by using the following eighth-note-based strum pattern:

There are a few things to note here.

- This is a four-measure pattern, with the only difference between measures 1–2 and 3–4 being the 16th-note flourish at the end of measure 2.

- You should strum this pattern down–up for the eighth notes throughout. For beat 4 of measure 2, strum down–down–up.

- The muted strums are created with the right hand—the same way they were in "Riptide" (see page 161).

Fingerpicking Pattern

There's also a fingerpicked part that occurs several times. For this pattern, assign *p* and the *i*, *m*, and *a* fingers to strings 4–1, respectively. In other words, use the following picking pattern:

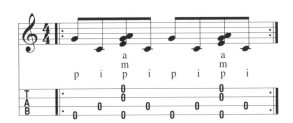

Note that an alternate voicing, with a C note on string 1 at fret 3, is used for the open F chord, which provides more continuity to the pattern.

INTERLUDE

For fun, in the interlude, we've arranged the flute part for ukulele as well, just in case you'd like to play along with someone else. The notes here are derived from form 2 of the C major pentatonic scale (with the tonic on string 2).

C Major Pentatonic

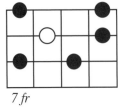

7 fr

5 Years Time

By Charlie Fink

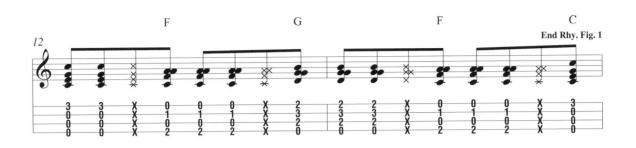

1. Uh, well, in

Verse
Uke 2: w/ Rhy. Fig. 1 (2 times)

five years' time, we could be walk-ing 'round ___ a zoo ___ with the

sun shin-ing down o-ver me and you. And there'll be love in the bod-ies of the

el-e-phants, too. ___ And I'll put my hands o-ver your ___ eyes, but

Chorus
Uke 2: w/ Rhy. Fig. 1 (2 times)

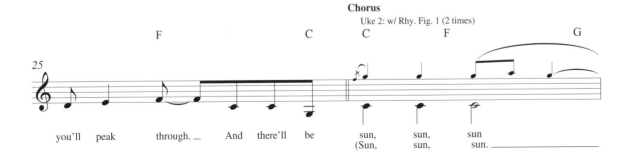

you'll peak through. ___ And there'll be sun, sun, sun
(Sun, sun, sun. ___

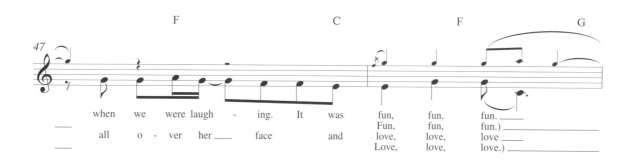

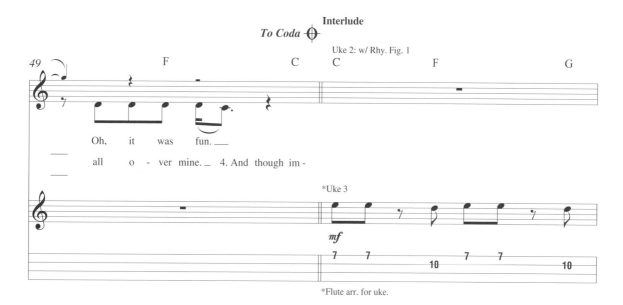

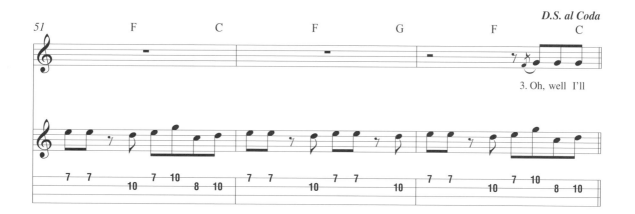

CHAPTER 18

"TONIGHT YOU BELONG TO ME"

What's Ahead:

- Loads of moveable jazz chords!
- New chord forms
- Triplet strum flourishes
- Chord-melody style

One of the most commonly played songs on the uke—largely thanks to the tender performance by Steve Martin and Bernadette Peters in the 1979 comedy film *The Jerk*, and more recently Eddie Vedder, who covered the song on his 2011 album *Ukulele Songs*—"Tonight You Belong to Me" is a delightful standard written in 1926 by Billy Rose and Lee David. Although Steve Martin is an accomplished musician (most notably on the banjo), jazz ukulele player Lyle Ritz actually performed the ukulele for the scene in the movie, and that's the version we'll look at here.

Lyle actually played in the same configuration as Vance Joy did for "Riptide"—baritone reentrant tuning on a tenor uke. We want to play the same voicings he used because they're so amazing, not to mention instructive (you'll get a huge workout with your moveable jazz chords!), but since we're playing it on a standard uke (not baritone tuning), this version will be a 4th higher. The original version was in G♭ (or F♯) major, so our version will be in B major. However, you'll be learning the same chord shapes that Lyle used. So, if you play this arrangement on a uke in baritone reentrant tuning, it will sound just like the version from the movie.

CHORDS AND RHYTHM

The chords here are played in typical jazz uke style, using a swung-eighths feel, with a mixture of eighth notes and quarter-note staccato rhythms. Lyle also throws in a few triplets to mix it up, and he occasionally slides into chords from a half step below. You learned most of the chords used here in Chapter 14, but there are a couple that you haven't seen yet, so let's take a look at those.

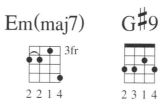

INTRO RIFF

Lyle creates a catchy little intro riff that reappears several times in the song. It's based on a B6 form strummed in a triplet rhythm and then slid up and down a half step. This is followed by another B6 form in a lower position. Notice how this creates a little melody on the top of the chords. This is a classic example of *chord-melody style*.

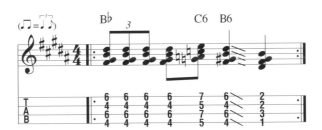

Be sure to note all the rhythmic variations and the articulations (staccato, half-step moves, etc.) throughout the song, as they all add to the character and charm.

Tonight You Belong to Me

Words by Billy Rose
Music by Lee David

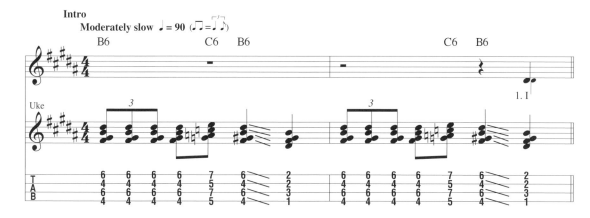

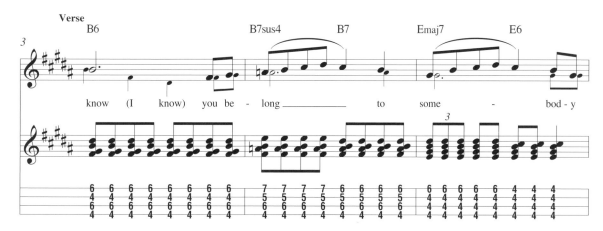

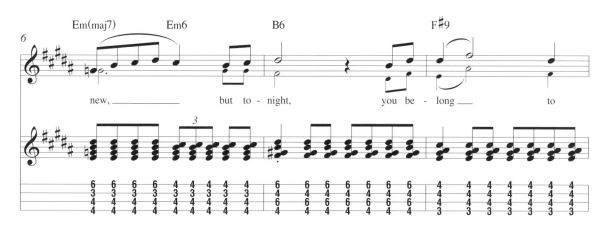

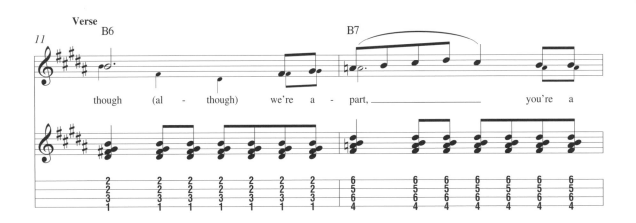

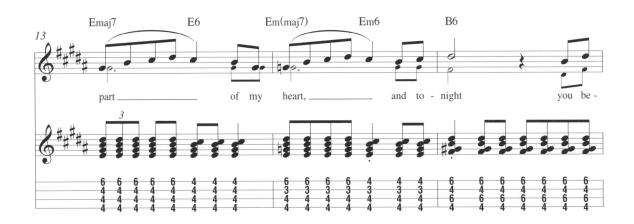

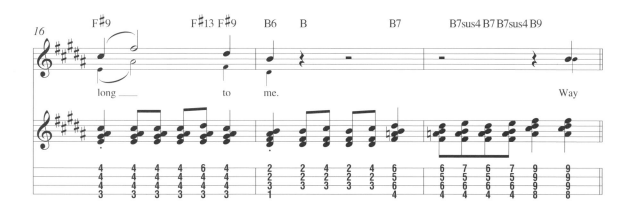

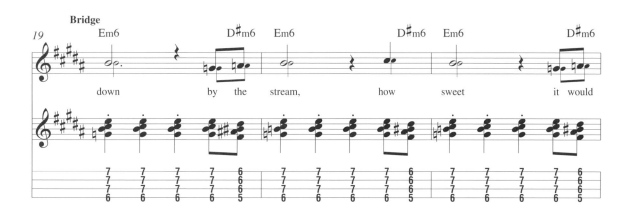

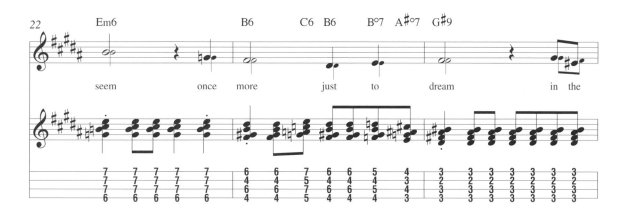

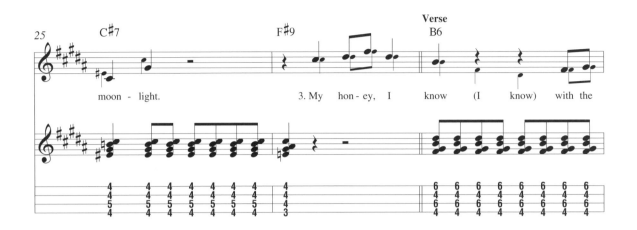

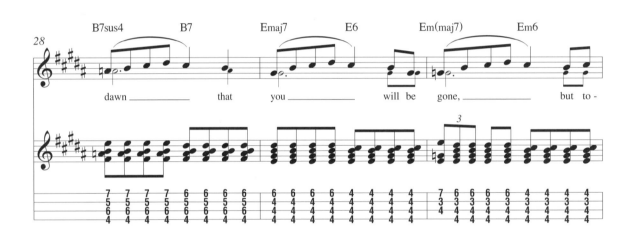

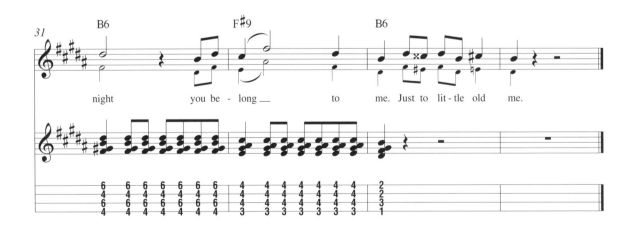

CHAPTER 19
"IN MY LIFE"

> ### What's Ahead:
> - Thumb-brushed chords
> - Pinching technique
> - Creative use of open strings and higher fretted notes

Jake Shimabukuro rose to international fame in 2006 because of a video in which he played "While My Guitar Gently Weeps" in Central Park. Evidently, he's quite the Beatles fan, because he's performed arrangements of several more Fab Four songs since then, including his gorgeous rendition of "In My Life," which appeared on his 2007 EP *My Life*. He also covered "Here, There, and Everywhere" on that same album.

Replete with delicate fingerpicking, beautiful chord voicings, and a gorgeous tone, the song marks a fitting conclusion to our studies in this book. Unlike much of his repertoire though, this arrangement is accessible to those of us who can't dedicate five hours a day to the instrument for years on end! Jake keeps this arrangement interesting the whole way through, treating each "verse" differently by varying the textures and harmonies. Note also that Jake is joined by a bass on the original recording.

SECTIONS A AND B

Jake begins in free time (no strict tempo) by stating the phrase that ends the chorus, fingerpicking throughout and mostly using the pinch technique to pair melody notes with lower notes. There are a few delicately strummed chords as well, which he strums with his thumb nail for a crisp sound. By the way, the wavy vertical line positioned next to some of the chords in this arrangement tell you to slowly brush through the notes of the chord, instead of using a typical quick strum. You can slowly brush through with a thumb or finger, or you can use the fingerstyle method of plucking each in a rolling, arpeggio-like motion.

Section B begins the song proper, picking up on the actual intro of the song as it appears on the Beatles recording. He's mostly just stating the melody here—granted, in 10th position, so it's a little crowded—adding a harmony note to the end of each phrase and treating the double stop to subtle vibrato.

SECTIONS C AND D

Section C coincides with the first verse, and Jake uses a fairly sparse texture here, mixing melody notes with thumb-strummed chords at first. At measure 17, he reaches the point in the phrase that he began with in Section A, and the treatment is similar: He combines pinched double stops with single melody notes and the occasional strummed chord.

There are a few very nice chord voicings in this section that are worthy of closer inspection.

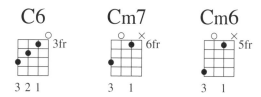

Section D is basically a repeat of Section B.

SECTIONS E AND F

For Section E, which would be verse 2, Jake abandons the earlier texture and plays a bit busier, goosing the song's momentum. He begins a fingerpicking pattern in mostly eighth notes, mixing open strings and higher fretted notes in creative manners. At this point, the melody becomes a bit more ghost-like. It's not stated outright as before; instead, it's only briefly glimpsed in certain spots. Since he doesn't settle into one continuous pattern, feel free to experiment with different right-hand fingerings to see what works best here.

There are a few dramatic rhythms here as well, including the quarter-note triplets, in which three quarter notes are fit into the space of two beats. An easy way to visualize this is by breaking each beat into eighth-note triplets and then accenting every other note.

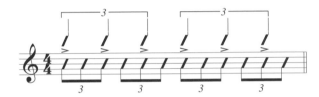

Section F essentially repeats Sections B and D, with the exception of a descending melody that leads back into Section C via the D.S. direction.

In My Life

Words and Music by John Lennon and Paul McCartney

Gearing Up

CHAPTER 20

SO MANY UKES, SO LITTLE TIME!

What's Ahead:
- Types of ukuleles
- Tonal considerations
- Shopping for a ukulele
- Electric ukuleles

Whether you're looking for your first uke or just looking to upgrade and/or add to your collection, this chapter will help make sure your next purchase is a wise one. If you're looking for an inexpensive model just for fun, or you want to get your dream uke custom built, there are plenty of options out there through which to weed. While this is ultimately a good thing, because it increases the chance of finding your perfect instrument, it can be daunting at first. So let's get some basic information under our belt that will help us determine what it is we want in a ukulele.

TYPES OF UKULELE

Sizes

There are four popular types/sizes of ukulele. From smallest to largest, we have *soprano*, *concert*, *tenor*, and *baritone*, typically ranging in size from 21 to 29 inches. In addition to these, there are other, less-common types, including the *pocket* (or *piccolo*), *bass*, and *contrabass*. Pocket ukes usually measure a mere 16 inches, while contrabass ukes span 32 inches.

Soprano (or "standard")   Concert   Tenor   Baritone

Aside from tone—the larger the instrument, the more bass response it has—size can play a big factor in playability too, particularly with those who have large hands. So it's always a good idea to get your hands on different sizes and try them out before you fall in love with one. You may love the way your friend's soprano sounds, but if you have big fingers, that just may not be in the cards!

Tuning

As mentioned earlier, soprano, concert, and tenor ukes are usually tuned G–C–E–A (reentrant tuning), although the tenor is often tuned to low G as well. A baritone ukulele is tuned the same as the first four strings of a guitar: (low to high) D–G–B–E.

The pocket uke is usually tuned two octaves above the baritone, but in reentrant tuning. So it's D–G–B–E as well, but the D string is tuned up an octave.

The bass ukulele is tuned exactly like a bass guitar: E–A–D–G. And the contrabass, which is quite rare, is tuned an octave below that! Both of these instruments are a bit quiet acoustically and sound much more impressive when used with a pickup and plugged into an amp.

Construction Materials

Most ukuleles are made from wood, but some inexpensive ones are made from plastic, and others are made from other composite materials. The very inexpensive wooden ukes are usually made from plywood laminate and, as is to be expected, the tone suffers. However, if you just want to dabble on the uke to see if you're interested and don't want to commit to anything serious yet, they can be had for a steal—around $30 or $40. You do get what you pay for, however, so we recommend always trying an instrument in person, as sometimes the very cheap models are set up so poorly that they won't even play in tune. If you can't try one in person, try to read all the reviews you can.

A step up from those models will usually get you a sapele, spruce, acacia, or mahogany body. All-solid wood construction improves tone, and these models usually start at around $100 and go up from there. Koa is one of the most traditionally used woods for ukes, revered for its tone and beauty, and those models will usually start around $250. Just as with most things, you can generally pay what you want to pay for something, and the price for custom-made ukes from the likes of Kamaka Ukulele or Mya-Moe can easily soar into the thousands. Needless to say, those models are usually reserved for only the most dedicated of players.

The audio for this book was recorded with a Kremona Coco Tenor ukulele, which is a beautiful instrument crafted with a solid cedar top and solid Indian rosewood back and sides. It also features a bone nut, a mahogany neck, and comes with a hardshell case and a KNA UK-1 detachable piezo pickup. At $599, it's a serious step up from the more entry level ukes without breaking the bank.

Kremona Coco Tenor Ukulele

TONAL CONSIDERATIONS

It should be mentioned that seemingly small things can make a noticeable difference in tone. The first of these is the strings. Budget-priced ukuleles will often be strung with very cheap strings when they ship from the factory. Changing these to a nice set of Aquila or D'Addario strings, which will run you around $10, can make a huge difference in tone. Not only that, but the instrument's intonation—it's ability to play in tune—can improve vastly as well. We'd recommend putting new strings on any new uke unless you know for sure that quality ones have been used.

The other big factor, aside from wood type, is the size of the instrument. The smaller the body, the less bass it can project. Therefore, a well-made soprano instrument will tend to sound a bit "skinnier" than a well-made tenor even though they're tuned the exact same way. Again, this is why it's a great idea to physically go to a store and trying playing the same thing (same chords or melodies) on each different size to see what sound and size suits your fancy.

ELECTRIFY YOUR UKE!

Another big decision you'll need to make is whether or not your ukulele will need to be electric (i.e., have a pickup or built-in microphone system that will allow you to plug it into an amplifier or P.A. system). If you plan on playing with a band or with several other instruments, this may be a requirement; otherwise, you'd have to rely on always being miked, and that could backfire.

Acoustic-Electric Models

Many instruments ship from the factory with a pickup installed and an output jack that doubles as a strap pin. Ukes of this type are often designated as "acoustic-electric" models. The price of these generally starts a bit higher than acoustic-only models, with the most inexpensive ones costing about $100 or so.

The cheaper models may have nothing more than a passive onboard pickup with no controls, but most models will feature an onboard "preamp" with multiple features. These can include a built-in tuner, a volume control, and a two- or three-band equalizer. Most of these models require a 9-volt battery to operate, which is usually drained only when the instrument is plugged in. Many feature a battery indicator as well, so you'll get a warning before it dies on you.

Ibanez UEWT5E
acoustic electric tenor ukulele

Aftermarket Pickups

If you happened to buy an acoustic ukulele and love the tone but have the need to electrify it, you still have several options. You can purchase a pickup and have it installed (or, if you're handy, do it yourself). For all intents and purposes, it will then be just like an acoustic-electric you buy at the store, with the exception that it most likely won't have an onboard pickup with the built-in tuner or other bells and whistles. There are two basic types in this regard: *active* and *passive*.

Active Pickups

An active pickup requires power to operate. All of the acoustic-electrics with built-in preamps contain active pickups, which is why they use a battery. Most active pickups, such as the Fishman Matrix Infinity, use a 9V battery. It also features volume and tone controls, which are mounted just inside the soundhole.

Fishman Matrix Infinity ukulele pickup

Passive Pickups

A passive pickup, on the other hand, requires no power whatsoever. These mostly come in two types: *under-saddle piezo pickups* and *soundboard transducers*. The first consists of a thin strip that lays underneath your saddle, while the second one is usually a small, disc-shaped device that sticks directly to the soundboard.

KNA UK-1 passive pickup

Installing a piezo pickup usually requires drilling a hole in your saddle slot. The pickup end slides through that hole and lays beneath the saddle, while the other end connects to the output jack inside the body. However, there is a piezo design by Kremona that allows you to simply slide a thin piece of wood under your string knots (if your ukulele uses a tie bridge similar to most classical guitars). The strip also features a female jack on the end of it, allowing you to run a plug straight from it to your amp/P.A. Therefore, no modification to the instrument is necessary.

The soundboard transducer does not require any modification, although you may need to remove a bit of adhesive residue that's left on the soundboard after removing it. Usually, neither system will feature any onboard volume control, so you'll have to make any adjustments on the amp itself. For this reason, many people using a passive pickup will run their uke into a volume pedal, such as the Boss FV-500H. This will allow you to at least control the volume locally.

Boss FV-500H volume pedal

Amplifiers

If you've got a cord dangling from your uke, you'll need a place to plug it in. There are two basic options: "direct" into a P.A. system or into an acoustic amplifier. If you run direct, you're usually leaving it up to the soundperson to get the sound right. Sometimes this works, and sometimes not so much. But it's certainly easier than lugging an amp around.

If you'd like more control over your sound, or you'd like to play amplified at home, then you'll need an amplifier. Amps that are designed for acoustic instruments produce a clean tone, as opposed to

Fishman Loudbox Mini Acoustic Amplifier

electric guitar amps, for example, which are often designed to produce varying levels of distortion. Therefore, in a pinch, you can make do with a keyboard or bass amp if you have one lying around, both of which are usually designed to produce a clean sound as well.

There are many brands of acoustic amplifiers available, and they will most likely provide the best tone and the best assortment of sound-shaping features. Check out models by Fishman, Behringer, Yamaha, Marshall, Boss, and Fender for good values. Since they're often designed for the singer/songwriter in mind, many of them feature two channels: one for the instrument (with a 1/4-inch jack) and one for vocals (with an XLR mic jack). It's not uncommon for them to feature built-in effects like reverb or delay as well, in addition to EQ controls and other goodies such as a line-in jack for MP3 players, etc. Prices range from about $75 or so up to $700 or $800 and more.

CHAPTER 21

CHANGING STRINGS AND OTHER ROUTINE MAINTENANCE

> **What's Ahead:**
> * How to change strings
> * Cleaning your ukulele
> * Storing your ukulele

Since we recommended in the last chapter that you should put new strings on your uke upon buying one, it seems only fitting that we should tell you how to do that. We'll also share some tips on cleaning and storing your instrument.

CHANGING STRINGS

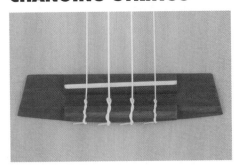

Before changing strings, you first need to deduce what type of bridge you have. Most ukuleles have a *tie bridge*, which is the same style found on most nylon-string (classical) guitars. The telltale sign of this bridge is the knots you see across the bridge, as the strings are literally tied to the bridge.

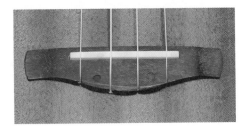

Another type of bridge is known as a *slotted bridge*. This will have slots carved into the bridge for each string. The strings are secured by tying a knot on one end of the string and securing it under the slot.

Changing Strings on a Tie Bridge

Let's start with the tie bridge, as that's still the most common bridge you'll find. This can seem a bit daunting at first because it just seems a little… sketchy. Are we really going to just "tie" this string to the bridge? Yep! Believe it or not, it works very well. However, there is a trick to it; in other words, just any old knot may not hold up. There's a set method that's stood the test of time…

Attaching the String at the Bridge

1. Begin with string 4. Make sure you have the correct string (always double-check!) and then pass the end through the neck-side hole in the bridge until about two inches are sticking out from the opposite side.
2. Bring the short end over the bridge and loop it under the long portion. Next, bring it back to the bridge and secure it by looping it under, over, and under again. This may take a bit of practice, so don't worry if you don't get it right at first. Just undo the knot and start again.
3. Once you've got the knot right, hold on to the short end while you pull up the slack toward the headstock.

Attaching the String to the Tuning Peg

1. Turn the tuning peg so that the hole is lined up with the string, then pass the string through it. Tighten the tuning peg so that the string has moved 90 degrees to the left.
2. While applying tension to the string, bring it back around the opposite direction (passing through the straight-on alignment it started with) and push it under the string, near the nut.
3. Pull up on the string with tension, binding the string against itself on the tuning peg.
4. While continuing to apply tension to the string, tune it up to pitch.
5. Repeat the same process for string 3. For strings 2 and 1, reverse the directions in steps 1–3.
6. Once you've got all the strings on, you can clip the excess off both ends of the string with a pair of wire cutters. Be extra careful not to damage your instrument!

Changing Strings on a Slotted Bridge

The slotted bridge is a bit easier than the tie bridge, and it works equally well. More and more slotted bridges are appearing on uke models all the time.

Attaching the String at the Bridge

1. Tie a simple knot at one end of the string. Repeat the process to create a larger, double-knot structure.
2. Feed the string through the slot, securing the knot behind the slot.
3. Pull up the slack of the string toward the headstock.

Attaching the String to the Tuning Peg

This procedure is the same as with the tie bridge.

CLEANING YOUR UKULELE

After playing for a good while on your uke, you may notice that it's not quite as shiny as it used to be. Or, if you're gigging often under hot stage lights, it won't take long at all for some grime to build up beneath your strumming arm and along the fretboard.

Cleaning is a fairly straightforward procedure. Often, all it takes is a slightly damp rag and a bit of elbow grease. Once you've scrubbed off the grime, use a clean dry cloth to wipe up any remaining moisture. Some people prefer to use a type of fretboard cleaner to help shine up their frets. It's inexpensive and will last a while.

For those who want to go the extra mile, there are guitar polish products that can be used on the body and fretboard as well. It's up to you to determine whether it's worth it or not. Some cleaning kits come with a polishing cloth, which is nice.

STORING YOUR INSTRUMENT

Obviously, if you want your uke to remain in tip-top shape, you should store it safely when not in use. It doesn't take much to cause a permanent scar, especially if you have young kids running around the house. If you have a hardshell case, that's the best spot for it, hands down. A well-padded gig bag is a nice second option. The operative word being "well-padded," because a flimsy, one-layer nylon gig bag doesn't offer much protection at all if it takes a tumble.

Ibanez IUBT541 POWERPAD
ukulele gig bag

Alternatively, you can mount a ukulele hanger on your wall (again, beyond the reach of toddler fingers if there are any in your home), which allows you to conveniently store it safely for temporary periods. They're inexpensive and easy to install.

Gator Wall Mount
ukulele/mandolin hanger

SECTION **7**

Who's Who

CHAPTER 22
TEN GROUNDBREAKING UKULELE PLAYERS

> ***What's Ahead:***
> * 10 highly influential ukulele players

Here, we'll take a look at 10 ukulele players who have inspired countless others to carry the uke torch that burns brightly today. They'll be listed in chronological order.

CLIFF EDWARDS (1895–1971)

Cliff Edwards was perhaps known best for his enormous 1929 hit "Singing in the Rain," as well as being the voice of Jiminy Cricket in Walt Disney's *Pinocchio* cartoon from 1940, which contained the classic "When You Wish Upon a Star." But he was also an extremely accomplished ukulele player and did much to spread the instrument's popularity throughout the '20s and '30s with his many on-screen performances. Edwards was inducted into the Ukulele Hall of Fame in 2000.

Photo Courtesy Photofest

ROY SMECK (1900–1994)

Nicknamed "The Wizard of the Strings," Roy Smeck was arguably the uke's first widely known virtuoso (he also played banjo, guitar, and steel guitar). He got his start on the Vaudeville circuit in the early '20s and, not being a great vocalist, developed his flashy style of uke playing to compensate. This included, among other things, playing the uke behind his head, with his teeth, and with a violin bow. He can even be seen tapping on the uke, Eddie Van Halen-style, in videos decades before the rocker even picked up a guitar.

ARTHUR GODFREY (1903–1983)

A charismatic radio announcer and entertainer, Arthur Godfrey—a.k.a. "the Old Redhead"—was an accomplished vocalist and ukulele player who entertained millions on various radio and TV programs throughout the '30s, '40s, and '50s. He was a smooth crooner with nimble fingers on the uke, and his songs "Ukulele Song" and "For You" are both fine examples. Godfrey was inducted into the Ukulele Hall of Fame in 2001.

Photo by Bettmann/Getty Images

Photo by Silver Screen Collection/
Hulton Archive/Getty Images

GEORGE FORMBY (1904–1961)

George Formby was a highly successful British actor and musician who ruled the '30s and '40s on both stage and screen. Known for his light-hearted songs performed on the uke, he became England's highest-paid entertainer for a time. Possessing a solid singing voice and exceptional adeptness on the instrument, he is arguably the most influential uke player in history. He was inducted into the Ukulele Hall of Fame in 2004.

EDDIE KAMAE (1927–2017)

Eddie Kamae was a Hawaiian ukulele virtuoso best known for his work with the group Sons of Hawaii. He taught himself to play by listening to the radio station and trying to play along, using a uke that his brother found on a bus. Eddie had a unique right-hand technique that combined thumb-strumming with fingerpicking. He founded the Ukulele Rascals, the first professional all-ukulele act, in 1948, and he was one of the first players to pluck chords and melodies simultaneously. Kamae was inducted into the Ukulele Hall of Fame in 2001.

Photo by Alvis Upitis/Getty Images

HERB OHTA (1934–)

Also born in Hawaii, Herb Ohta (a.k.a. Ohta-San) began playing ukulele at age 9, after being taught a few chords by his mother. At the young age of 12, he met Eddie Kamae and became the virtuoso's student. Over the years, Ohta-San has developed an incredibly versatile style and is accomplished in traditional Hawaiian, as well as jazz, pop, romantic, and orchestral music. His son, Herb Ohta, Jr., is following in his father's footsteps and is an accomplished player as well.

JOE BROWN (1941–)

Born in England, Joe Brown has enjoyed a musical career spanning over five decades. A multi-instrumentalist who, in addition to the uke, plays guitar, banjo, mandolin, fiddle, and sings, he's influenced leagues of musicians throughout his career, including the Fab Four themselves. In fact, George Harrison (another uke enthusiast) was Brown's best man at his wedding in 2000. Joe delivered several heart-felt performances at the Concert for George tribute show in 2001. A "musician's musician" with a knack for anything stringed, Brown has taught more than a few players a thing or two.

Photo by Judy Totton

ISRAEL "IZ" KAMAKAWIWO'OLE (1959–1997)

Born in Hawaii and a lifetime resident of the island, "Iz" was almost singlehandedly responsible for the latest uke resurgence that's continued to this day. On his 1993 album *Facing Future*, he included a last-minute cover of "Somewhere over the Rainbow" combined with "What a Wonderful World." The song caught fire and appeared in several films, including *K-Pax*, *Meet Joe Black*, *Finding Forrester*, *50 First Dates*, as well as numerous TV series, including *ER*, *Scrubs*, *American Dad!*, *Glee*, *South Pacific*, *LOST*, and *Storm Chasers*, among others. *Facing Future* has gone on to sell over a million copies and is the best-selling album of all time by a Hawaiian artist.

Photo by Debra L Rothenberg/Getty Images

JAKE SHIMABUKURO (1976–)

Known in some circles as the "Jimi Hendrix of the Ukulele," Jake Shimabukuro is a next-level virtuoso that simply owns the instrument. Though he had been well known in his homeland of Hawaii and Japan for years, he rose to world-wide prominence in 2006 when someone posted an anonymous YouTube video (without his knowledge) of him performing "While My Guitar Gently Weeps." One of the first viral videos on YouTube, it has since been viewed over 15 million times. Since then, Jake has been dazzling audiences all over the world with his unparalleled virtuosity, continuously redefining what's considered possible on the instrument.

JAMES HILL (1980–)

Another virtuoso that's pushing the instrument into new horizons, Canadian-born James Hill is a consummate performer on the instrument and fluent in many styles, including jazz, pop, blues, classical, and traditional Hawaiian, among others. Although he's the least well known on this list, and has mostly garnered attention on YouTube, that's bound to change in the years to come, as his skill on the instrument is matched by very few. As well as being an engaging performer, James is also a champion of ukulele education and runs a popular site called The Ukulele Way. Keep your eyes and ears out for this rising star of the uke!

Photo by Kris Connor/Getty Images for Make Music Day

CHORD CHART

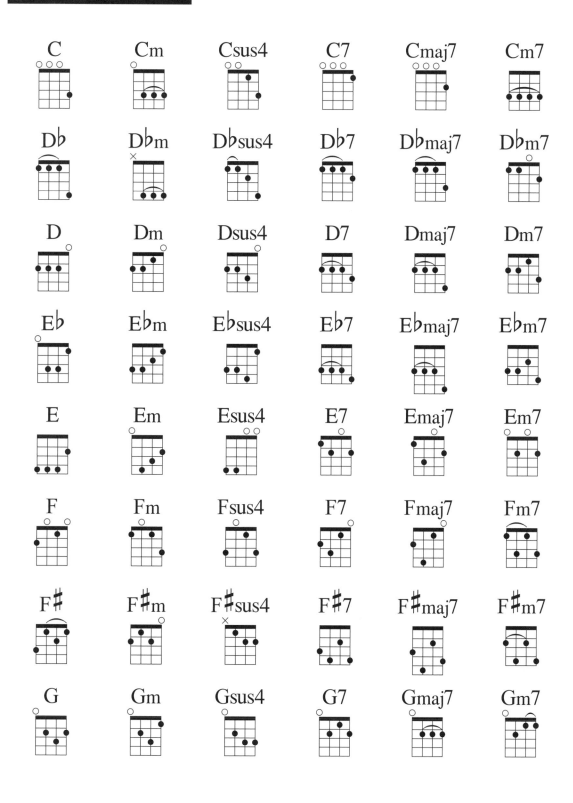

CHORD CHART (CONTINUED)

A♭	A♭m	A♭sus4	A♭7	A♭maj7	A♭m7

A	Am	Asus4	A7	Amaj7	Am7

B♭	B♭m	B♭sus4	B♭7	B♭maj7	B♭m7

B	Bm	Bsus4	B7	Bmaj7	Bm7

SCALE CHART

Major

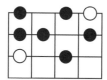 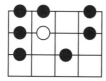

Minor

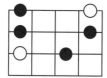 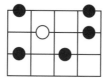

Major Pentatonic

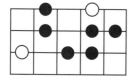 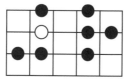

Minor Pentatonic

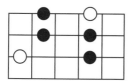 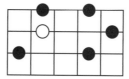

Blues

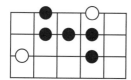 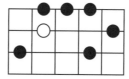

Mixolydian

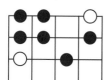 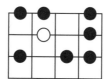

ABOUT THE AUTHOR

Chad Johnson is a freelance author, editor, and musician. For Hal Leonard, he's authored over 80 instructional books covering a variety of instruments and topics, including *Ukulele Aerobics*, *Baritone Ukulele Aerobics*, *How to Play Solo Ukulele*, *Guitarist's Guide to Scales Over Chords*, *How to Record at Home on a Budget*, *The Hal Leonard Acoustic Guitar Method*, *Ukulele for Kids*, *Teach Yourself to Play Bass Guitar*, *How to Build Guitar Chops*, *Play Like Eric Johnson*, and *Bass Fretboard Workbook*, to name but a few. He's a featured instructor on the DVD *200 Country Guitar Licks* (also published by Hal Leonard) and has toured and performed throughout the East Coast in various bands, sharing the stage with members of Lynyrd Skynyrd, the Allman Brothers Band, and others. He works as a session guitarist, composer/songwriter, and recording engineer when not authoring or editing and currently resides in Denton, TX (North Dallas) with his wife and two children. Feel free to contact him at *chadjohnsonguitar@gmail.com* with any questions or concerns and follow him at *www.facebook.com/chadjohnsonguitar*.

ACKNOWLEDGMENTS

Thanks so much to my family—my lovely wife, Alli, and my two wonderful children, Lennon and Leherie—for always reminding me what's most important in life by just being who they are.

Thanks to my parents, Mike and Kay, and my sister, Mika, for not throwing out my instruments while I learned to play during my awkward young teen years.

Thanks much to all the fine folks at Hal Leonard for doing what they do so well. It's always a pleasure to work with y'all.

And thank you to all the amazing ukulele players of past and present who continue to inspire me every day.